Kerry Kern

Siberian
Huskies

Everything About Selection, Care,
Nutrition, Behavior, and Training

BARRON'S

2 CONTENTS

HISTORY OF SIBERIAN HUSKIES

Siberian Huskies were bred by the Chukchi, indigenous people who inhabit the Arctic coastal region of northern Siberia.

The Chukchi Dog

For more than 1,000 years, a tribe of people known as the Chukchi have inhabited the Arctic coastal region of northern Siberia—a land where the extremes of winter make life a daily challenge just for survival. The Chukchi were hunters and sometimes used teams of dogs to pull whales and other large carcasses onto the ice and back to the village. It is there that the Chukchi dog, the progenitor of today's Siberian Husky, was developed.

Over many generations of breeding, the Chukchi developed the breed of dog that most suited their needs. Although their permanent home was inland, the Chukchi hunters worked primarily along the coast, with seal as their main food source. The hunters' catch was not so heavy as to require large dogs capable of pulling great weight. Instead, the Chukchi hunters needed a dog that could withstand extended exposure to the low temperatures, that could pull a light-to-moderate load

quickly over long distances, and that could expend a minimum amount of energy in the process. The less energy the dog used on its work, the more it had left to protect it from the weather. There are two types of Chukchi: Reindeer and Coastal. The Coastal Chukchi bred and raised the dogs from which many of today's Siberian Huskies descended. Research indicates that the Chukchis maintained the purity of their sled dogs through the nineteenth century and that these dogs are the sole and direct ancestors of today's Siberian Huskies.

Quick, small working dogs that were docile and intelligent enough to work in teams proved most suited to the work and terrain. They had to be hard, eager workers that had enough common sense and dedication to their task to keep from constantly tangling themselves in the lines of the sled. The Chukchi so valued their dogs that they often took them into their homes as guardians, and as companions for their children. This, no doubt, accounts for much of the gentleness in the Siberian Husky personality.

The Chukchi dog's most important trait was its instinct and desire to run, seemingly endlessly. Because of its moderate size, it was able to run far and fast, but it could not pull much weight. Therefore, teams of dogs were required to pull the hunters' loads. The Chukchi were able to breed a dog that combined all these traits, and today's Siberian Husky traces to those dogs.

The fate of the Chukchi dog—and the birth of the Siberian Husky breed—are tied to several historical events, primarily in Russia. In the eighteenth century, Russian Cossacks began a march across Siberia to conquer the land and to attain all of its resources, primarily fur. Most people living in this northern area were primitive tribal groups who were unable to compete with the advanced weaponry of the invading Russian army. The Chukchi people were able to withstand conquest, however, because their sled dogs always kept them ahead of the advancing military forces. Although they could not fight, they could run—efficiently. The Chukchi were accustomed to the Siberian weather; the Russian soldiers were not, and they suffered great losses.

The Chukchi actually forced the Cossacks to abandon their quest to conquer all of northern Siberia. The Chukchi lured the Russian forces into a mountain pass, in which all escape routes were blocked. Using only sharpened rocks and spears, the Chukchi inflicted substantial casualties on the Russians, who subsequently withdrew from the area.

The Chukchi people and their dogs existed peaceably in Siberia for many years after this conflict. By the close of the nineteenth century, the Chukchi dog had been discovered by Alaskan traders, imported into the Seward Peninsula of the Alaskan Territory, and renamed the Siberian Husky. This importation proved very important for the survival of the breed. The first recorded import of these dogs was in the fall of 1908 by William Goosak, a Russian fur trader.

In the early 1900s, the monarchy in Russia was overthrown and replaced by a Communist regime, vowing to do away with all "bourgeois" and elite aspects of Russian life. By the 1930s, the forces of Communism reached the Arctic North. Because Chukchi dogs were highly revered and desired by the Chukchi people, those members of the tribe who bred and maintained the finest dogs had assumed a leadership position and a measure of wealth. Such people were viewed as hindrances to the forces of collectivization, and most were imprisoned or killed. In just a few years, the Chukchi dog breed all but disappeared from Siberia.

Dog Sledding Begins

Unlike the breed's fate in Russia, the Siberian Husky was taking hold in Alaska. Dog sledding had become not only a means of transportation, but also a popular sport for the adventurers who had journeyed north in search of gold. Local races quickly evolved into large events with numerous entries. A lawyer named Albert Fink undertook the task of regulating the dogsled events and helped formalize the sport, as well as founding the Nome Kennel Club.

The dogs used in the early races were primarily Alaskan sled dogs, originally bred to haul freight. They were larger and stronger than Siberian Huskies, but were not as quick.

They were, however, well adapted to the terrain and had great competitive spirit. In 1909, Goosak first entered a team of Chukchi dogs in the All-Alaska sweepstakes sled race from Nome. Goosak hired William Thrustrup—a skilled musher—to drive the team on the 408-mile course. Few thought these dogs could compete against teams comprised of the larger Alaskan sled dogs.

On the first day of the competition, a severe snowstorm erupted that blinded the mushers with blowing snow. Most teams gave up, but three remained steadfast in the competition—two were made up of Alaskan dogs that knew the trail well, and the third was Thrustrup and his Chukchis. The dogs had never been on the trail before, but somehow they stayed on course. While the two other teams stopped to rest in Candle, Alaska, Thrustrup's team continued on and headed back to Nome.

Thrustrup's team grew tired, so he let them rest one at a time on his sled. Both Alaskan teams completed the race in around 82 hours, and Thrustrup's team came in at approximately 89 hours. While the team did not win the race, they attracted a lot of attention to the breed.

For the 1910 Sweepstakes, a musher named Charles Fox Maule Ramsay traveled to Siberia and returned with 60 Chukchi dogs. He picked what he believed to be the best 12 of these dogs for his sledding team and hired another musher to drive the second-best team of 12 from the stock. Ramsay then hired John "Iron Man" Johnson to drive a third sled comprised of the remaining dogs. Exceeding everyone's expectations, Johnson's team of "underdogs" won the race and set a record time of 74 hours.

The first sled driver to gain notoriety on the sled dog circuit using Siberian Huskies was Leonhard Seppala, a Norwegian who had emigrated to Alaska early in the twentieth century. He inherited a ragtag team of Siberians that had originally been scheduled to drive explorer Roald Amundsen to the North Pole. When the expedition was canceled because of World War I, the dogs were given to Seppala. Over the next few years, Seppala's Siberian Husky teams beat all racers throughout the Northwest. His Siberians were all but unbeatable in the annual 25-mile Borden Cup Race in Nome.

In January 1925, Seppala and his Huskies earned a place in history. During that winter, an epidemic of diphtheria broke out in Nome, and local doctors did not have adequate supplies of the required diphtheria serum. At the time, Nome was connected to the lower territories only by telegraph; the nearest railroad station was more than 650 miles east, at a small outpost named Nenana. Seppala was asked to go and collect the serum by dogsled—in a race against time. Seppala and his team traveled along the northern shore of Norton Sound, part of the Bering Sea—some of the most treacherous sections of Alaska's wilderness. A relay team of 15 sleds and dogs was sent west from Nenana with the serum to meet Seppala, as the world waited. On the day Seppala met up with the relay team at Shaktoolik (after mushing nearly 170 miles) he had already traveled more than 40 miles in blizzard conditions; he retrieved the serum and immediately headed back to Nome, posting another 80 miles before resting briefly. His team of 20 dogs amassed nearly 350 miles in this journey. The teams from the south ran relays of approximately 20 to 50 miles each, and contributed greatly to the success of this mission.

News reports of the feats of Seppala's dogs brought great acclaim to the breed. Demand in the United States reached a fever pitch in 1927, when Seppala raced his dogs in New England. Because Alaskan breeders were unable to fill the requests they received, many interested fanciers imported dogs directly from Siberia. Through the efforts of these fanciers, the breed was soon firmly established in the United States. In 1930, the breed was granted recognition by the American Kennel Club (AKC). Today's Siberian Husky that is bred specifically for sled work is slightly stockier and taller than the specimens seen in the show ring.

Modern Dogsled Races

Like the early Chukchi hunters, Alaskan breeders have worked hard to produce the breed of dog most suited to the northern climate and the requirements of modern dogsled racing. Breeders have used Alaskan Village Dogs, Siberian Huskies, and other native dogs to produce a strain of sledding dogs now termed Alaskan Huskies. Today, Siberian Husky teams compete in many aspects of dogsled racing, but they have limited success against Alaskan Husky specialists in the traditional long-distance hauling races.

The Siberian Husky specializes in races involving speed, agility, and maneuverability. Common classes at dogsled races include those for three dogs running 3 miles, six dogs running 6 miles, eight dogs running 9 miles, and the unlimited class in which teams of up to 20 dogs race 14 or more miles. Middle-distance races (35 to 120 miles per day) are the Siberian's forte, as they require a fast trot. Sprint races typically involve dogs that are skilled in galloping, unlike the Siberian, which prefers a quick trot.

Training a Siberian Husky dogsled team is a year-round process. During the months when snow is not available, the dogs must still be conditioned, as weather permits. During warmer weather, the teams are worked on training sleds that are hooked up to All-Terrain Vehicles (ATVs). During this preparation, the dogs become accustomed to the harness and the weight they will need to pull, and, most importantly, they learn to work and run together as a team.

Today's most famous dogsled race, the annual Iditarod Trail Sled Dog Race from Anchorage to Nome, commemorates the historic journey of Leonhard Seppala and his Siberian Huskies as well as the other serum relay teams that assisted in the journey. The course is more than 1,100 miles and currently offers a purse of $560,000, with more than $50,000 going to the winner. A record time of a little less than 9 days was posted in 2002 by four-time winner Martin Buser.

Dogsled racing is monitored worldwide by the International Federation of Sleddog Sports, a coalition of sled dog racing associations and 18 member countries. Independent races, such as the Iditarod or Yukon Quest, are not monitored by the International Federation of Sleddog Sports (IFSS) but rather by private governing committees.

Historical Helpers

Siberian Huskies have enjoyed a storied history within the United States and have been utilized in many historic situations. Many Siberian Huskies were assembled and trained at the Chinook Kennels in New Hampshire for use on the Byrd Antarctic Expeditions, which began in 1928. In addition, many valiant Siberians also served in the Army's Arctic Search and Rescue Unit during World War II.

CONSIDERATIONS BEFORE BUYING

The decision to purchase a dog, especially a Siberian Husky, should be made only after you have evaluated the suitability of that breed to your home and daily life.

The Right Dog for You?

Siberians require weekly brushing, and new owners must be prepared to provide a daily outlet for exercise. Predatory instincts are strong, and so is the inclination to run, so Siberians should be supervised around small animals, both inside and outside of the home. The following questions may also help guide you in your evaluation:

Does owning a dog suit my lifestyle? A good owner must train the dog thoroughly in the basic commands and supply it with daily love, attention, adequate housing, and an outlet for its energy. The Siberian Husky is not a good breed for those who work long hours and leave their pets alone. To thrive, Siberians need companionship, ample space, and a good dose of exercise. Owners must make a lifelong commitment of personal attention and daily walks with the dog for approximately the next 11 to 15 years.

In addition, owners should consider the climate in which the dog will live. Although you can certainly keep a Siberian if you live in a warm climate, you will need to take extra care and precautions during the summer months.

Can I properly care for a Siberian Husky? A Siberian Husky can be quite expensive to maintain. Aside from the initial purchase price, which can range anywhere from $400 to more than $1,000, an owner must provide routine veterinary care, flea and heartworm preventatives, and an ample, nutritious diet. Such costs are considerable and constant throughout the dog's life.

Is a puppy wanted by everyone in the household? Despite good intentions, owners sometimes find that other family members view the household pet—especially a puppy—as a nuisance. Because this usually spells disaster for the dog, think carefully and discuss how owning a dog may affect the existing household routine and the members of the home before you commit to pet ownership. Similarly, an adult Husky—in his enthusiasm to jump and greet a visitor—can easily knock a child or an elderly person over, possibly into furniture or on to hard surfaces. You must consider the ability of all members of the household to live with the dog. Some breeders recommend that these dogs—while loving toward all—should not be placed in homes with children younger than three years old.

Another factor to consider is the propensity toward allergies in family members. Many people are allergic to dog or cat hair, and while Siberians are not among the breeds most linked with allergic reactions, a serious pet dander allergy should make you reconsider your choice of pet.

Do I really want a puppy? Puppies require a significant amount of attention, monitoring, and training. They will need frequent walks and access to the outside during the housetraining process. There will be accidents, and there may be damage from chewing. An older dog may be more appropriate for those who cannot be home during the day.

Do I have the time to exercise a Siberian Husky? More than any other consideration, willingness to exercise the Siberian is of utmost importance for owners. Merely giving them access to a fenced yard is not enough. These dogs need at least one lengthy walk daily, with a workout of some kind along the way. Although Siberian Huskies are lovable and friendly, they should not be living with sedentary owners. A Siberian Husky should never ever be placed on an outside leash and left for long periods. If this is your plan for exercising your dog, choose another breed.

Purchasing Your Siberian

If you have answered "yes" to all the preceding questions, the search for your Husky can begin. Over the years, Siberian Husky breeders have worked steadfastly on protecting against careless overbreeding, which often happens after a breed becomes popular. Despite this breed's popularity, locating a large number of quality Siberian Husky puppies is not as easy as you would think. Most Siberian owners and breeders do not produce a large number of litters. They are careful about which dogs are bred and where the puppies are placed.

Show Dog, Sled Dog, or Pet?

To find the best source for your dog, you must first decide what functions the dog will be expected to fulfill. Are you looking for a show competitor, a sled dog, or a companion? If you are looking for a potential winner in competitive contests, you need to do thorough research and make a careful selection.

Selecting a puppy destined to be a show dog is always a gamble. Most puppies are purchased at eight to ten weeks of age—a time of rapid development. What the dog will look like when mature cannot be accurately assessed at this time, only predicted. Selections made while a Siberian puppy is still growing (until approximately 12 to 15 months) are "best guesses"

and should therefore be based on pedigree and the breeder's knowledge of how his/her dogs mature. Because a preliminary evaluation of breed type can be made more accurately at four to six months of age, hold off purchasing a show prospect until then, if possible. "Show-quality" puppies will be expensive, so a careful selection is imperative.

If you want a sled dog, you should locate an established kennel that actively participates in the sport. Do not be surprised if they have little available stock, however, because these breeders generally will keep the puppies with best potential for themselves until they can more thoroughly evaluate the puppies for speed and desire at a later age. For novice sledding enthusiasts, most well-bred Siberians should fill the bill for desire and pulling ability.

People who want a pet Siberian Husky have many options. If there is a good Siberian kennel in your area, preferably one that produces show winners, ask if they have any pet-quality dogs available. These puppies or slightly older dogs will be well-bred, quality Siberians that have been eliminated from competitive status for some minor fault that makes them unsuitable for the show ring. With such dogs the pedigrees of both dam and sire are known, and the puppies have been raised during the formative stages by knowledgeable people. The price of such puppies usually will be from several hundred dollars and up.

Regardless of where you purchase your Siberian puppy, you should obtain a purchase contract, litter registration, and copies of all genetic screening results. No one should buy a Siberian puppy without copies of both parents' genetic tests and registrations, including documents from the Orthopedic Foundation for

Animals (OFA), which focuses on hip dysplasia; the Canine Eye Registration Foundation (CERF)— a centralized, national registry of dogs certified free of heritable eye disease by members of the American College of Veterinary Ophthalmologists (ACVO); and the Siberian Husky Ophthalmic Registry (SHOR).

SHOR is a low-cost alternative to CERF that documents Siberians who have been inspected for heritable eye diseases by an ACVO eye specialist. Upon receipt of a clear ACVO exam report form, the dog will be issued a SHOR number. (For more information on heritable eye diseases, see page 72.)

Although some Siberian breeders sell their animals to pet stores, most that breed for the show ring or for competition do not.

Pet Quality

Pet-quality Siberian Huskies can also be bought from pet stores or neighborhood litters. If you are considering a pet-store dog, be sure to find out about its parents' genetic history, where the puppy was purchased, and get as much information as possible about his initial care. Although quality pet stores will deal only with knowledgeable and reputable local breeders, there have been cases where unscrupulous shop owners have purchased dogs from "puppy mills" throughout the United States, where dogs are mass produced from whatever breeding stock is available. Quality should always be your primary concern, not easy availability. The price for a purebred dog from a pet shop will often be the same as pet-quality and sometimes show-quality dogs from private kennels.

Neighborhood litters are a common source of pet-quality dogs, and the purchase price generally is quite reasonable. You should ask to see both the mother and father's registration papers before you buy any puppy. Without this documentation, the puppy's litter will be ineligible for registration with the American Kennel Club (AKC). If the breeder cannot supply these papers, you cannot be sure you are buying a registerable purebred—and the purchase price you pay should reflect this. With random breedings such as this, the parents are likely to be from diverse genetic backgrounds. Although the resulting puppies will almost always be fine representatives of the breed, there is little chance that you are buying a future conformation champion.

A small number of Siberians find homes through the work of national rescue leagues, which stay in close contact with shelters and retrieve most purebred Siberian Huskies, should they turn up. They then try to place the dog in a suitable home. Reputable rescue organizations and shelters will require new owners to sign a contract accepting the dog "as is," and they will typically have the animal spayed or neutered before adoption. The names and addresses of local, regional, and national Siberian Husky organizations and their corresponding secretaries can be obtained by writing the AKC (see page 93 for the address). The AKC magazine, *Purebred Dogs: American Kennel Gazette,* is published monthly and contains a breed column, a list of advertising kennels, articles on all aspects of dog care, information on upcoming shows, and lists of recent winners.

Remember: Not all breeders are working for the betterment of the breed. Be sure to check credentials, and stay clear of anyone who seems more interested in profit than the welfare of this breed.

Evaluating a Puppy

Regardless of how you intend to use your Siberian Husky, he should be carefully evaluated for general health and essential breed characteristics. When possible, begin your evaluation before the prospective puppy is even born. It is prudent to make sure that both the sire and dam have been checked for canine brucellosis (an infectious disease caused by the *Brucella canis* bacteria), hip dysplasia, glaucoma, XPRA (the mutated disease gene responsible for progressive retinal atrophy, or PRA), and juvenile cataracts. Start your evaluation at the beginning, because the care a litter receives during the first few weeks of life can have lifelong effects. The living quarters must be clean, fairly spacious, and parasite-free.

There should be signs that the owner has interacted with puppies during the early days, not just left them alone with the mother in some secluded spot.

Look not only at a puppy, but at his litter as a whole. Purchasing the puppy from a poor litter is a risky endeavor. Ask the breeder why the parents were selected for breeding and whether they had been checked for a predisposition toward hip dysplasia.

The Parents

You usually can get a pretty good idea of a puppy's probable size and type by looking at both the dam (mother) and sire (father). Often only the dam is available, as the sire may be from another kennel. Don't be too critical of the dam's outward appearance, however. She has just endured the whelping and nursing of her litter, so she may appear thin or run down. The owner probably will have a prepregnancy picture that can give you a better indication. Acceptable behavior for the dam would be to act aloof, calm, and stable; she may be curious or friendly toward you, but she should not be penalized for being a bit reserved or standoffish. This is a breed trait. She should be responsive to her owner and should respond to assurances that all is well.

Try to get as much information as possible regarding the sire. Ask if this breeding pair have ever been mated previously. If yes, you may be able to see some of the maturing dogs from a previous litter or ask for the name and phone number of an owner of one of these dogs. This is especially important if you are purchasing a show prospect.

Overall Appearance

When evaluating an eight-week-old puppy, first look at his overall appearance, bearing in mind that a growing puppy is likely to appear somewhat awkward and out of balance—different skeletal areas grow at different rates. He should be vigorous and plump (but not bloated, which can indicate a worm infestation). A thriving puppy is clean and pleasant smelling, his eyes are clear and not runny, and there is no discharge in the ears.

The Siberian puppy should appear compact, with a deep chest and level back. He should move effortlessly and be quite active. Siberians are not timid and should respond cheerfully when engaged into play. A well-socialized puppy will not be intimidated by this, although he may be a little reserved. He should submit to gentle handling and allow you to physically inspect him. A slight variation in size among littermates and between the sexes is normal, and the largest puppy should not be deemed most desirable simply on this account. Important breed characteristics are the almond-shaped eyes and the "fox" tail. The "masks" that many Huskies have around the face are present from birth and may intensify with age.

What Age Is Best?

Although there is no set answer to the "best age" question, most breeders believe that puppies should be at least seven weeks old before being separated from their litter. At eight to twelve weeks of age, puppies are in a developmental stage known as the "human socialization period." This is the best time for a puppy to learn how to live happily with humans. A dog that remains with his litter and receives little contact with humans during this time will have his primary bond with dogs rather than humans.

It is also vital that the puppy is not removed much *before* eight weeks of age—during the canine socialization period. During the weeks spent with his pack, a dog learns how to get along with other animals. If removed too early,

the poorly socialized dog may react aggressively or submissively when he meets other dogs. The end result can be fighters or "fear biters" who easily are upset and prone to unexpectedly lashing out at other dogs and people. Puppies produced in the "puppy mills" often suffer from improper socialization because they are removed too young from their litter to arrive at retail outlets by eight weeks of age.

The greatest advantage of purchasing a puppy (besides being able to play with it during its most adorable stage) is that the owner is able to influence the dog's interaction with his environment. A Siberian Husky should never be placed on an outside leash and left for long periods. If this is your plan for exercising your dog, choose another breed. If you select an older Siberian puppy, be sure he has been raised with lots of human contact and interaction rather than left solely with his litter. Such a dog will be able to adapt quickly to a new home with humans, whereas a dog that has always been surrounded by his pack will feel isolated by such a change.

The Purchase Agreement

Hopefully, selecting your Siberian puppy has been an enjoyable experience. You must now formalize the agreement by putting all the terms of the deal in writing. Be precise and list not only the purchase price, but also the terms of the guarantee and what documentation will be supplied.

To guarantee that the puppy is healthy, most breeders will allow new owners a certain number of days to have the puppy examined by their personal veterinarian. Get the specific terms of the deal in writing—a verbal promise will get you nowhere legally. The agreement should specify whether a sick dog will be replaced with a healthy puppy or if the purchaser's money will be returned.

When dealing with a kennel or pet store, the new owner of a purebred Siberian Husky should receive the puppy's AKC registration application at the time of the purchase. The application should include the names and AKC numbers of the sire and dam, information on the litter from which the puppy was whelped, and the name and address of the person to whom ownership is being transferred. The new owner must list two possible names for the puppy and complete all missing information. Processing the paperwork should take about three to four weeks, if all is in order.

Established breeders most likely will have registered the puppy's litter with the AKC shortly after birth and should have received these applications prior to the sale of any of the puppies. If the application is unavailable, the new owner must get a signed bill of sale from the breeder that lists the breed, sex, and color of the puppy; his date of birth; and the registered names (with numbers) of the sire and dam. Without this information, the AKC likely will be unable to register the dog.

Kennels that breed Huskies strictly for show purposes may have some additional purchase terms. The breeder may want to be involved with the future breeding of the dog or may stipulate that he will be sold only on the condition that he is shown in competition for his championship. Such concerned kennels may agree to sell a pet-quality dog only on the condition that he not be bred and may even withhold registration papers until proof is supplied that the dog has been neutered. In exchange for such terms, the breeder often will offer an attractive selling price for the dog.

UNDERSTANDING SIBERIAN HUSKIES

Siberians are considered primitive dogs, as many of the "early" dog instincts are still prevalent.

Pack Behavior

Many theories state that the first doglike animals on earth date to around 600,000 B.C. Domesticated dogs date back nearly 20,000 years, with their closest recognizable ancestor being the wolf. During this time, life was extremely harsh, and food supplies were limited. These primitive animals learned the benefits of grouping together for survival. A pack behavior evolved, entailing various levels of hierarchy patterns among the dogs. The most assertive dog assumed the leadership position, leaving the other pack members to fall in line behind.

This pack behavior taught dogs the value of social cooperation and helped the progenitors of today's domestic dog and early man to form their first alliance—presumably as a result of a mutual need to hunt together for food. As time passed, man learned how to breed dogs selectively to attain certain goals: fast runners, good hunters, avid watchdogs. Such useful quali-

ties served humans well. Over time, a bond of friendship also arose, and the first dual-purpose dogs developed: workers and companions.

Behavior Patterns

Modern dogs have inherited many of the traits utilized by the earliest members of their species, though rarely are they called on to utilize these long-hidden survival instincts. Although pack behavior still exists, dogs have had to learn to adapt to the rules of the human pack. Domestication has tempered the aggressiveness that early dogs needed for survival, but through selective breeding many of the characteristics and traits that man found most useful survived.

Siberian Huskies originated in a land with some of the harshest weather on earth to serve their owners as sled dogs and companions. In other terrains, dogs of various structures and temperaments evolved to serve the particular needs of their owners. Even though many distinct breeds exist, all dogs share a common heritage and a basic means of expression, which is exhibited in their communication methods.

Hierarchy

If left to their own accord, when grouped together, unfamiliar dogs will instinctively begin to establish a hierarchy for this new pack. The most dominant dogs immediately will vie for top position. They will stand well up on their feet, snarl, and try to intimidate any perceived opponent. An inspection of the anal area generally is in order for each of the dogs. Fierce growling can ensue, as well as the raising of the hair along the spine, referred to as the "hackles." Occasionally a fight may break out, but this usually is short-lived, as one animal will recognize his vulnerability and yield to the more dominant dog. The emerging leader often is referred to as the "alpha" dog.

Such maneuvering for power also will occur between dog and owner, although more often this is a war of wits rather than a physical confrontation. If the human does not exhibit what the dog perceives to be proper leadership qualities, the dog will think he is entitled to rule his pack and will try to do so. Owners must be aware of this and exhibit an assertive, consistent manner when dealing with the dog—especially when willful disobedience occurs. The dog must understand that he is subordinate to *all* humans in his pack, not only one primary master, and this instruction should begin as soon as the puppy is introduced into the household. He already has been indoctrinated by his mother, the original alpha (that is, top dog), so he should learn quickly to accept his assigned place as pet—not leader—of the home.

Siberian Huskies are gentle dogs and not prone to viciousness. In a multidog household, however, some dogs instinctively may challenge the presence of other animals they believe are vying for the superior position in that pack.

In households where there are multiple Siberians, cooperative behavior may occur. Siberians will hunt as a pack and may team up to chew, dig, or destroy personal property if not well supervised. Acting up may also result from a mild case of jealousy, especially if an owner seems to favor one dog over others. On the whole, however, the Siberian Husky is so well mannered and amiable that all should get along peaceably.

Communication

Communication methods, such as vocalization, facial expression, and body language, are basically uniform among all breeds of dogs. Humans can learn to interpret more accurately the meaning of a dog's actions by being alert to what the dog's body language is showing (and also to what your body language and vocal tones are telling the dog). Your dog has a limited frame of reference. He must rely on the signals you give with your commands, vocal tones, and physical demeanor. Owners should pay attention to the differences among the various sounds the dog makes and the significance of the accompanying movements.

Body Language

A Siberian at ease will have a relaxed posture: his head and ears are up and his tail is at rest or moving slowly. When happy, the tail usually moves on a horizontal plane, the ears are up, and the dog may whine or give off some short barks. A dog inviting play often will drop his front to the ground while keeping his hindquarters up (and his tail will be wagging). When at attention, the dog's ears point more forward, the tail is more horizontal, and the dog appears more up on his toes.

An aggressive dog will have an angry expression, with his ears pointed directly forward or pulled against the side of the head, and he may bare his teeth and emit low growls. A fearful dog is perhaps the most dangerous. He does not look as menacing as the aggressive dog, but he is very unpredictable. The face is slightly tensed, and the ears are pulled against the head; the overall body position is lowered. If the dog feels threatened, he can lash out quickly from this position.

A submissive dog often is mistakenly thought to be a dog that is feeling "guilty." He assumes a lowered position, tail down and tucked under his belly, ears pointing back. He will avoid eye contact, and his eyes will look rolled down and whiter than usual. This dog is not feeling guilty (which is a human condition), but rather he is responding submissively to an authority more dominant than himself. In addition, a submissive dog may attempt to lick the mouth or hands of the dominant individual, roll onto his back, or even urinate as further indication of his submission.

Mood Indicators

A confused, upset dog may also assume a lowered stance, but he will not grovel or try to lick. Instead, he may pant rapidly, which is indicative of stress.

Facial expressions often can help an owner understand a dog's intent. Siberians are masters of "cute." They can look so sweet and innocent that it is hard to resist their charm.

The position and movement of the tail usually are good mood indicators. A Husky often carries his tail curled up and over his back rather than in the horizontal position that generally indicates contentment for other breeds. This position also can indicate excitement or heightened attention. A low-slung tail position indicates fear or apprehension.

The Owner's Role

Pay attention to the body language signals that your dog is giving you. Assess the

situation and respond properly. These are the actions of a leader in the dog's view.

A dog will respond to his owner primarily by how he interprets that person's vocal tone and body language. This response, and the few basic command words he has been taught, are all it has to work with. The owner must, in turn, show the dog what is expected of him by example.

Positive Reinforcement

Dogs learn to obey by positive experiences; they learn to fear by negative ones. The following scenario is a classic example of miscommunication: after discovering a housebreaking "mistake" on the carpet, the owner yells, chastises, or even hits the dog, which is now crouched low to the floor in search of a safe place to hide. The owner interprets the dog's actions to be signs that he knows he has done wrong and is showing his guilt. In truth, the dog is submitting to the master in an act of self-preservation. He hears loud, angry tones, sees an angry expression, and reacts with fear. He has not been given any reason to associate his actions with the master's reactions. Nothing has been resolved here. The dog is afraid and confused; the owner has done nothing toward eliminating any similar mistakes.

The best way to encourage a dog to learn and retain information is through positive reinforcement. To be an effective leader you must show the dog what he is expected to do, and praise him highly when the task is accomplished. If mistakes are made, the dog should be corrected promptly and again shown the proper action. When the action finally is completed, the dog should then be praised.

Many factors complicate this learning process. Some Siberian Huskies are more intelligent than others, making them more capable learners. Many Siberians are stubborn or easily bored by training procedures, making them less willing learners. Some owners are better trainers than others. Although differences abound, both dog and owner can establish a system that works for them if they are willing to commit to the process.

If you encounter problems, try to evaluate what the cause may be: Is the dog confused? Is he testing my authority? Am I making my commands clear? Can the dog do what I am asking of him? The answers to these questions will provide important clues to how well your dog understands your training program, and how you may need to alter your methods to achieve the best results.

Digging

Siberian Huskies love to dig, especially down through layers of snow. They often dig a body-size hole—their "nest"—and lie down contentedly in it. They also will dig into the ground, which is an annoyance. The resulting muddy paws and destroyed flower beds can irritate even the most mellow owner, so be aware and prepare. Don't plant flowers in the dog's exercise area, don't let the dog roam the flower garden without supervision, and consider protective fencing. Check the dog's feet for dirt when he enters the house. You've got to work out a balance, as the dog will dig and take great pleasure in it.

All fencing in the yard should be buried to a depth that exceeds the digging capability of the dog, or the fence can be mounted in a solid foundation. Some Siberians also display a curious habit of giving a quick dig and then circling in the immediate area they are about to lie down in. (When on your hardwood floor or carpeting, this can be a problem.) This action is a throwback to the primitive times when dogs needed to carve out a nest for sleeping to protect themselves from the elements. Again, take your dog's habits and instincts into consideration when deciding where the dog is allowed to roam and sleep.

Living with a Siberian

A Siberian Husky's good points heavily outweigh his minor peculiarities. No dog is more loving and beguiling than a Siberian. He has a great zest for life, has boundless love in his heart, and a mischievous spirit. He is beautiful, with friendly eyes. Although not prone to much barking, he will let off a characteristic howl when making himself heard.

Don't count on the Siberian to be an ardent watchdog. He likes people, even strangers, too much to take offense at intruders. Although he can be relied on to bark when he hears someone outside, this is more a welcoming yowl than a warning growl.

The Siberian has an independent streak that often surfaces during training. When disinterested, a Siberian will not feign excitement to please his owners. A wise owner must work around this by being a little more inventive than just following the textbook rules for training. When running is part of the routine, the Siberian is sure to perk up. Siberians love tag games and teasing. Use these games as other trainers would use tidbits to reward good work and more than likely you will keep the dog interested and learning—happily.

Companionship is vital in a Siberian's life. He will not do well alone. If he cannot have plenty of human attention, he must at least share his home with another dog to help him fill the hours until the owner returns. If left alone, he probably will become irrationally nervous and shy—traits foreign to the well-adjusted Husky. He also wants lots of exercise and time outdoors.

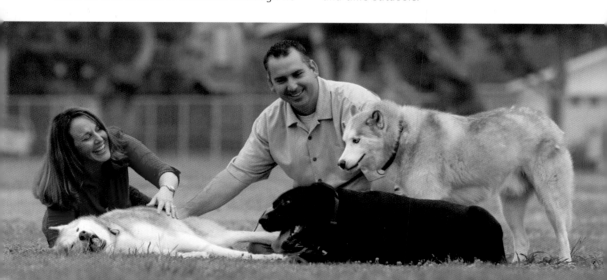

For safety, always remember that the Siberian will wander. He does not try actively to break away from his master; he just becomes enticed by any new sound or sight and will take off quickly after it. A Siberian can run very fast, and he is weak at sensing dangerous situations, such as approaching cars, open manholes, or deep trenches. Siberians will chase neighborhood cats, squirrels, and other "prey-like" stimuli. The breed is highly independent, has an innate predatory instinct, and will not necessarily come when called. They will run until they get tired—it's in their genes. Extra care is needed to make sure that your Siberian is in complete control when outside of the home. Always keep the dog on a leash when outdoors and let him loose only in well-fenced areas. Without fail, if you leave a gate open, your Husky will go exploring.

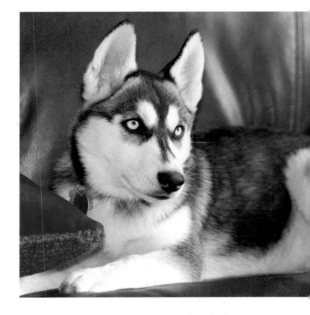

The Quality Siberian

The Siberian Husky descends from what is called the spitz group—the dogs of the extreme northern climate that typically had thick, shaggy coats, pointed muzzles, plumy tails, and an incredible ability to work hard under the most extreme conditions. Siberians did not descend from wolves. The other breeds in this group include the Alaskan Malamute, Chinock, Samoyed, Shiba Inu, Keeshond, and Finnish Spitz.

The Siberian is most often compared with the Alaskan Malamute. Although the Malamute has similar markings, he is a larger dog of heavier bone that excels at pulling heavy loads over long distances. The Siberian is built for speed and endurance. He has a moderately compact body, with a deep chest and very muscular loins. He weighs only up to 60 pounds (132 kg) and has great pulling strength for his size. He is, in fact, one of the smallest of the working breeds.

The Siberian exhibits a wide range of coat colors, including occasionally an all-white. Most have a striking mask on the face. His eyes may be either blue or brown, which makes it one of few breeds that have blue eyes as a desirable trait. Many Siberians have one blue and one brown eye, and this is perfectly acceptable and not to be penalized in the show dog.

Siberian Husky Standard

Following is the official breed standard for the Siberian Husky, as devised by the national breed club and accepted by the AKC. It defines the ideal Siberian Husky. Although few dogs could measure up point by point with all requirements of the standard, it is the guide by which dogs are judged and serves as the goal for dedicated breeders. As approved by the American Kennel Club, October 9, 1990, effective November 28, 1990.

General Appearance

The Siberian Husky is a medium-sized working dog, quick and light on his feet and free and graceful in action. His moderately compact and well-furred body, erect ears and brush tail suggest his Northern heritage. His characteristic gait is smooth and seemingly effortless. He performs his original function in harness most capably, carrying a light load at a moderate speed over great distances. His body proportions and form reflect this basic balance of power, speed, and endurance. The males of the Siberian Husky breed are masculine but never coarse; the bitches are feminine but without weakness of structure. In proper condition, with muscle firm and well developed, the Siberian Husky does not carry excess weight.

Size, Proportion, Substance

Height: Dogs, 21 to 23½ inches (53.3–59.7 cm) at the withers. Bitches, 20 to 22 inches (50.8–55.9 cm) at the withers.

Weight: Weight is in proportion to height. Dogs, 45 to 60 pounds (20.4–27.2 kg). Bitches, 35 to 50 pounds (15.9–22.7 kg). The measurements mentioned above represent the extreme height and weight limits with no preference given to either extreme. Any appearance of excessive bone or weight should be penalized. In profile, the length of the body from the point of the shoulder to the rear point of the croup is slightly longer than the height of the body from the ground to the top of the withers.

Disqualification: Dogs over 23½ inches and bitches over 22 inches.

Head

Expression: Is keen, but friendly; interested and even mischievous.

Eyes: Almond shaped, moderately spaced and set a trifle obliquely. Eyes may be brown or blue in color; one of each or parti-colored are acceptable. *Faults:* Eyes set too obliquely; set too close together.

Ears: Of medium size, triangular in shape, close fitting and set high on the head. They are thick, well furred, slightly arched at the back, and strongly erect, with slightly rounded tips pointing straight up. *Faults:* Ears too large in proportion to the head; too wide-set; not strongly erect.

Skull: Of medium size and in proportion to the body; slightly rounded on top and tapering from the widest point to the eyes. *Faults:* Head clumsy or heavy; head too finely chiseled.

Stop: The stop is well-defined and the bridge of the nose is straight from the stop to the tip. *Fault:* Insufficient stop.

Muzzle: Of medium length; that is, the distance from the tip of the nose to the stop is equal to the distance from the stop to the occiput. The muzzle is of medium width, tapering gradually to the nose, with the tip neither pointed nor square. *Faults:* Muzzle either too snipy or too coarse; muzzle too short or too long.

Nose: Black in gray, tan, or black dogs; liver in copper dogs; may be flesh-colored in pure white dogs. The pink-streaked "snow nose" is acceptable.

Lips: Are well pigmented and close fitting.

Teeth: Closing in a scissors bite. *Fault:* Any bite other than scissors.

Neck, Topline, Body

Neck: Medium in length, arched and carried proudly erect when dog is standing. When moving at a trot, the neck is extended so that the head is carried slightly forward. *Faults:* Neck too short and thick; neck too long.

Chest: Deep and strong, but not too broad, with the deepest point being just behind and level with the elbows. The ribs are well-sprung from the spine but flattened on the sides to allow for freedom of action. *Faults:* Chest too broad; "barrel ribs;" ribs too flat or weak.

Back: The back is straight and strong, with a level topline from withers to croup. It is of medium length, neither cobby nor slack from excessive length. The loin is taut and lean, narrower than the rib cage, and with a slight tuck-up. The croup slopes away from the spine at an angle, but never so steeply as to restrict the rearward thrust of the hind legs. *Faults:* Weak or slack back; roached back; sloping topline.

Tail

The well-furred tail of fox-brush shape is set on just below the level of the topline, and is usually carried over the back in a graceful sickle curve when the dog is at attention. When carried up, the tail does not curl to either side of the body, nor does it snap flat against the back. A trailing tail is normal for the dog when in repose. Hair on the tail is of medium length and approximately the same length on top, sides, and bottom, giving the appearance of a round brush. *Faults:* A snapped or tightly curled tail; highly plumed tail; tail set too low or too high.

Forequarters

Shoulders: The shoulder blade is well laid back. The upper arm angles slightly backward from point of shoulder to elbow, and is never perpendicular to the ground. The muscles and ligaments holding the shoulder to the rib cage are firm and well-developed. *Faults:* Straight shoulders; loose shoulders.

Forelegs: When standing and viewed from the front, the legs are moderately spaced, parallel and straight, with the elbows close to the body and turned neither in nor out. Viewed from the side, pasterns are slightly slanted, with the pastern joint strong, but flexible. Bone is substantial but never heavy. Length of the leg from elbow to ground is slightly more than the distance from the elbow to the top of withers. Dewclaws on forelegs may be removed. *Faults:* Weak pasterns; too heavy bone; too narrow or too wide in the front; out at the elbows.

Feet: Oval in shape but not long. The paws are medium in size, compact and well-furred between the toes and pads. The pads are tough and thickly cushioned. The paws neither turn in nor out when the dog is in natural stance. *Faults:* Soft or splayed toes; paws too large and clumsy; paws too small and delicate; toeing in or out.

Hindquarters

When standing and viewed from the rear, the hind legs are moderately spaced and parallel. The upper thighs are well-muscled and powerful, the stifles well bent, the hock joint well defined and set low to the ground. Dewclaws, if any, are to be removed. *Faults:* Straight stifles, cow-hocks, too narrow or too wide in the rear.

Coat

The coat of the Siberian Husky is double and medium in length, giving a well-furred appearance, but is never so long as to obscure the clean-cut outline of the dog. The undercoat is soft and dense and of sufficient length to support the outer coat. The guard hairs of the outer coat are straight and somewhat smooth-lying, never harsh nor standing straight off from the body. It should be noted that the absence of the undercoat during the shedding season is normal. Trimming of whiskers and fur between the toes and around the feet to present a neater appearance is permissible. Trimming the fur on any other part of the dog is not to be condoned and should be severely penalized. *Faults:* Long, rough, or shaggy coat; texture too harsh or too silky; trimming of the coat, except as permitted above.

Color

All colors from black to pure white are allowed. A variety of markings on the head is common, including many striking patterns not found in other breeds.

Gait

The Siberian Husky's characteristic gait is smooth and seemingly effortless. He is quick and light on his feet, and when in the show ring should be gaited on a loose leash at a moderately fast trot, exhibiting good reach in the forequarters and good drive in the hindquarters. When viewed from the front to rear while moving at a walk the Siberian Husky does not single-track, but as the speed increases the legs gradually angle inward until the pads are falling on a line directly under the longitudinal center of the body. As the pad marks converge, the forelegs and hind legs are carried straightforward, with neither elbows nor stifles turned in or out. Each hind leg moves in the path of the foreleg on the same side. While the dog is gaiting, the topline remains firm and level. *Faults:* Short, prancing or choppy gait, lumbering or rolling gait; crossing or crabbing.

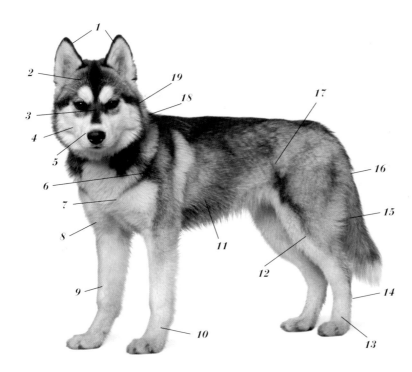

The anatomy of a
Siberian Husky:
1. ears
2. skull
3. stop
4. cheek
5. muzzle
6. shoulder
7. chest
8. forequarters
9. foreleg
10. front pastern
11. rib cage
12. stifle
13. rear pastern
14. hock
15. hindquarters
16. tail
17. loin
18. withers
19. neckline

Temperament

The Siberian Husky is friendly and gentle, but also alert and outgoing. He does not display the possessive qualities of the guard dog, nor is he overly suspicious of strangers or aggressive with other dogs. Some measure of reserve and dignity may be expected in the mature dog. His intelligence, tractability, and eager disposition make him an agreeable companion and willing worker.

Summary

The most important breed characteristics of the Siberian Husky are medium size, moderate bone, well-balanced proportions, ease and freedom of movement, proper coat, pleasing head and ears, correct tail, and good disposition. Any appearance of excessive bone or weight, constricted or clumsy gait, or long, rough coat should be penalized. The Siberian Husky never appears so heavy or coarse as to suggest a freighting animal; nor is he so light and fragile as to suggest a sprint-racing animal. In both sexes, the Siberian Husky gives the appearance of being capable of great endurance. Obvious structural faults common to all breeds are as undesirable in the Siberian Husky as in any other breed, even though they are not specifically mentioned herein.

Disqualification

Dogs over 23½ inches and bitches over 22 inches.

CARING FOR SIBERIAN HUSKIES

Siberians are extremely people-oriented, and they adapt well to the "human pack."

The Siberian Husky's recent popularity can be traced to numerous factors: his beauty, intelligence, ease of care, loving personality, hardiness, and workmanship, among others. Siberian Huskies excel as companions, but can also be trained to do many types of work (although guard dog duty is not definitely compatible with their people-loving nature).

Adaptability is the key to Siberian Huskies. They do well in both urban and rural settings; no climate is too extreme, as long as precautions are taken to maintain a healthy temperature. The top requirement for owners is to provide the dog with companionship—both human and canine—from his earliest days. This is the key to a good beginning, one which will let the puppy develop to its fullest potential.

Getting Settled

Even though Siberian Huskies have been used throughout the breed's history as workers, they have traditionally been raised as companions as well. This tractable, personable nature helps Siberian puppies make the transition from litter to new home with relative ease.

Before you bring your new puppy home, there are a few basic supplies to purchase.
• a food and a water bowl (heavy enough not to slide while the dog is eating or drinking);
• a high-quality puppy food (preferably the brand it has already been eating);
• a crate with bedding;
• a puppy-size collar and lead;
• a grooming brush and comb; and
• a few safe chew toys.

The house should be puppy-proofed in much the same way as you would for a toddler. Although it might seem silly, the best way to check for potential dangers is to get down and inspect each room from the puppy's level. Remove not only all items that can be chewed or swallowed, but also any heavy items that are stored low enough to fall on an inquisitive puppy. Exposed electric cords are obvious targets during teething. Open staircases are very hazardous and should be closed off to ensure that the puppy will not fall down the stairs.

During his first few days in the home, the puppy will get his first—and probably lasting—impression about his new territory and owners. These early days should be enjoyable for the puppy. The owner should pay careful attention to the dog's actions and movements at all times. All members of the household will have to adapt to the new arrival. Be mindful of the puppy's whereabouts, as one of the most common injuries to a puppy is from being stepped on while under foot. Allowing the puppy to play too exuberantly is also dangerous. Jumping from too great a height can result in broken legs, hips, or shoulders.

Discipline

Living strictly among humans is probably new for your puppy. He will have to learn from the start that although there will be lots of love and fun experiences, there also will be corrections and discipline. A Siberian Husky puppy can be so charming that the owner will overlook his misdeeds. Don't be fooled into thinking that a puppy cannot learn while young, or that trying to get the puppy to obey at an early age will ruin his spirit. A puppy can understand that some actions displease the owner and must be stopped. The puppy's dam has probably made it perfectly clear to her pups that there are limits to acceptable behavior, and when rules are broken there is a correction. The owner must step into this leadership position. Dominance over the dog should be established while young and should be reinforced daily. Some easy ways to exert control are to keep the dog guessing and responding to the owner's wishes. Move the dog's food bowl every once in a while, and pick it up momentarily during an occasional meal; when you give it back, praise the dog for his patience. Put the dog on his back and rub his belly and feet thoroughly. This is fun and establishes control. It also helps to desensitize any discomfort he may have of having his feet touched, which will help when clipping his nails in the future. (See page 58 for more on nail care.) Change his sleeping place, even if just for a night or two, to prevent the dog from developing territoriality. Little actions like these mean a lot in imprinting the lesson that humans are in control.

It is never too early to begin teaching your puppy what is acceptable and what is unacceptable. Much learning occurs during the first days and weeks. An owner can help shape the behavior of the adult dog to come through careful monitoring and positive correction.

The First Day

When making the arrangements to pick up the puppy from his breeder, try to choose a time when you have several days free to devote to welcoming the dog to his new home (such as the beginning of a weekend or during a vacation period). Morning is best, because that gives you the whole day to spend with the dog before he spends his first night away from his littermates and dam. The more time you spend with the puppy, the easier the transition. If you bring a young puppy home one day and leave him alone the next while you go off to work or school, the puppy may feel abandoned and subsequently have a difficult time adjusting to his new home.

Speak to the puppy in soft, low tones and treat him gently. An easy way to enhance bonding is to frequently get down on the floor with the puppy. By playing with the puppy on his level you will seem more like a friendly, rather than a towering, figure. Even though Siberian puppies are pretty rough-and-tumble, rough play is not recommended during the first few days. The puppy needs lots of attention and praise to help him feel reassured, comforted, and encouraged during these trying times.

As soon as you get home with the puppy, show him where his food and water bowls are located, and take him to the elimination area—it's never too early to begin housetraining! Show him his sleeping quarters. You can then let the dog roam about his new home and explore on his own (while you monitor from

nearby). Until reliably housetrained, a puppy should be confined to his crate whenever he is not being supervised directly.

The puppy will need his own sleeping area. While young, a small bed, sleeping box, or crate is recommended (see more on crates in Housetraining on page 91). This area will be the pup's new "den," and he should return (or be returned) to it for all sleeping. Bring the puppy to this area whenever he seems to be tiring. The sleeping area plays an important role in fostering a sense of security.

Although the crate may seem strikingly like a cage, your Siberian puppy will see it as his very own place. Do not let your own feelings become an obstacle to the use of this genuinely helpful training device.

Because a puppy of seven to nine weeks of age should still be receiving four meals a day, he will soon need to be fed. He will be nervous, bewildered, and may even have a slightly upset stomach, so reduce his suggested ration by about one third. Afterward, the puppy may explore a bit more, or he may settle down for a nap. During the first four months of life, puppies need frequent rest and will exhibit great swings in energy levels—periods of great activity will be followed closely by periods of sound sleep.

Because puppies easily are overstimulated, try to make the first few days fun but not exhausting. This often is easier said than done with the exuberant Siberian puppy. Everything is new and exciting, and the puppy may push himself beyond his endurance. Learning the voice and appearance of just the members of the immediate family is quite a chore for the puppy. Try not to bring in a continuous stream of new faces to meet the new puppy. Introduce neighbors over the next few weeks or in short meetings while out for a walk. All meetings between young children in the household and the puppy should be closely monitored, and the children should be instructed on how to gently pet, lift, and handle a puppy.

Other Pets

Meeting the other pets in the home can be quite stressful for all involved. If possible, give the puppy a little time to adjust to the new surroundings before meeting other animals. Delaying this too long may unnerve the other pets, however, as they surely will sense the new presence. Make sure all the pets are strictly supervised and able to be restrained. Although adult Siberian Huskies rarely react aggressively toward puppies, anything can happen under such circumstances. Praise the animals highly throughout the meeting, showing the established pet lavish amounts of affection. If any animal should growl menacingly or lunge at the other, you immediately must correct with a stern warning and a shake of the neck, and remove him from the room. A new puppy is sometimes thought to be a threat to the household order, but this competitiveness usually eases with time.

Although a Siberian Husky is less likely to immediately go after a cat than many other breeds, there may be some aggressive behavior. Dogs and cats do not immediately understand each other's body language, and either animal's reactions can range from curiosity to apprehension to open hostility. A Siberian that has been raised with cats generally will be peaceable toward them throughout his life. (My Reba always greeted each cat she met with a gentle nudge of the nose; this continued throughout her life despite more than a few scratches across the snout.)

Siberian puppies raised in a house with an indoor cat can generally maintain an amicable relationship, but the same is not guaranteed in an outdoor setting, where the predatory instincts may kick in. Adult Siberians brought into a house with a cat are to be considered unreliable and should be closely supervised. Small house pets—such as gerbils, hamsters, and pet birds—are always in danger, and interactions should be closely monitored, if not forbidden altogether.

Siberian Huskies are traditional pack animals used to living with several dogs. Occasionally, jealousy can be a problem in multidog households. Owners must try to give equal affection to all pets in the home to avoid competition and resentment. This is important especially when introducing a puppy, as it is easy to be so concerned with making the puppy feel comfortable that the other pets feel neglected.

Children

Although Siberian Huskies are by nature loving toward children, some do not adapt well to the rough treatment children can inflict. For the safety of all concerned, a Siberian Husky should never be left alone with an infant. Even a docile dog such as this can be an imposing figure; merely being stepped on can be dangerous to small children.

The First Night

Because puppies are not used to being alone, the first few nights may be frightening for them. Most will whimper or cry. It is important to establish a routine right from the start—the experience of the first few nights will set a pattern for the nights to come. Unless you plan on letting your dog sleep on your bed or in your room with you in the future, don't begin that pattern. Consistency is vital, and you shouldn't let the puppy do something one week that is forbidden the next.

Most puppies will need comforting during the first few nights, but do not overdo it. Bring the puppy to his sleeping area, pet him and talk soothingly to him for a few minutes, and then go.

If you make it seem matter-of-fact, you will do more for the puppy than if you draw it out. If the puppy raises a fuss after a few minutes, return to reassure him. Do not linger there or remove him from the sleeping area. If you pick him up, the puppy will sense your uneasiness and learn that if he howls long enough you will come and get him. Soft, soothing background music or a hot water bottle under his blanket to imitate the mother's warmth often helps relieve the puppy's tension enough to let him fall asleep.

The puppy should settle down more easily over the next few nights. Remember to praise the puppy and lavish lots of attention on him first thing each morning to reward good behavior over night.

Daytime Care

To flourish, a Siberian Husky puppy will need lots of attention and companionship. He should not be expected to stay alone for more than short periods. Left alone for great lengths of time, a puppy will feel abandoned. Most maladjusted adults began as lonely or poorly treated puppies, and little can be done later to counteract the effects of a poor beginning. The end result often is a high-strung dog with undesirable habits, such as tension chewing, howling, or scratching. A Siberian Husky, in particular, does not do well when left to entertain himself.

When leaving the home for an extended time, try to arrange to take the puppy with you. If this is impossible, try to leave the dog with someone he is acquainted with. With modern work schedules, this often is not possible. Regardless, a puppy has exercise, elimination, and socialization needs that must be attended to during the day. As the dog matures, he will be able to be alone for longer periods; however, while a puppy, you may need to hire someone to care for him. In many cities there are professional dog walkers or sitters, and school-age children often are willing to come to your home and care for your pet. Siberians are people-oriented and rarely adapt well to extended separations. It is not fair to keep this breed if you cannot attend to this particular need.

Socialization

Puppy socialization classes, often called "Kindergarten Puppy Training," are informative sessions held by local dog clubs to help introduce both owner and puppy to some basic training and discipline techniques. These classes do not include formal obedience training, but instead focus on showing owners some basic handling skills and housetraining methods.

The trainers also discuss such things as canine nutrition and health care, and provide background information on how a puppy learns and understands. An emphasis is usually given on teaching the owner proper techniques for establishing his or her place as leader and gaining control over the puppy right from the start. A good trainer should evaluate each dog and base the lessons on what is shown by the animal. To communicate effectively, an owner must behave in a manner the puppy understands. If the dog does not receive the cues he expects from a leader, he will not feel compelled to obey. Puppy socialization classes help produce effective owners and well-mannered puppies.

Puppy socialization classes also are valuable because they expose the puppy to new people, dogs, and surroundings. The dog's ability to know how to handle himself around other animals is vital. Siberian Huskies are peaceable by nature and rarely are antagonistic when encountering another dog. How the other dog will react is always an unknown, however, so the owner must be alert to recognize all possible dangers. Early lessons in socialization will help the dog to learn self-control and how to handle new situations. It is an owner's responsibility to ensure this proper behavior. Puppy socialization classes instill a sense of accomplishment and self-confidence in the dog, and these components are vital in developing a positive attitude toward training.

Outdoor Exercise and Housing

No breed enjoys the outdoors more than a Siberian Husky. They have flourished in some of the coldest, harshest areas on earth. Although most Siberian Huskies in the United States are kept as companions in the home, they also can adapt to being housed in a kennel building—provided there is plenty of human and canine companionship during the day. Siberians are much too people-oriented to be kept strictly as kennel dogs.

Siberian Huskies should be given plenty of time outdoors. They thrive when allowed to romp, and their quick bursts of speed are a sight to behold. Siberians run straight and fast, not in a circling pattern. They need adequate amounts of exercise to release tensions that may accumulate when confined indoors. The release they get from being outdoors keeps them more relaxed in the home and helps thwart such negative habits as tension chewing or howling.

A Doghouse

Siberian Huskies are very happy to spend a considerable amount of time outdoors. But no matter how hardy the breed and how impervious to the elements this breed seems, they still require proper protection from the elements. Doghouses can be constructed to provide adequate shelter against heat, cold, and dampness. It must be well insulated and large enough to let the dog fully stretch out, but not too large to lose warmth. The entrance should be just large enough to allow the dog to enter easily. A doghouse with a hinged top is easiest to clean.

The doghouse must be in a shaded area during the hot months and a sunny area during the cold months. It should be mounted on platform risers or placed on blocks to stand several inches off the ground so that there is no direct contact with the soil. Do not position the doghouse directly against a fence. Although Siberians are not noted climbers, they are good jumpers. Placing a doghouse in this way gives the dog the opportunity to climb on it and jump to freedom.

Fencing

Any area that Siberian Huskies are allowed to roam in freely must be properly fenced, preferably to a height of 5 or 6 feet (1.5–1.8 m). Siberians are easily distracted by the "call of the wild" and think they are impervious to any possible danger from passing vehicles. Because of these traits, it is extremely dangerous to allow them access to open areas. A secure run is a good solution, because it lets the dog roam but also keeps him in safe confinement. Siberians also like to dig, so the fence should be buried slightly to thwart any possible chance of tunneling under it. Some Siberians even have the desire and ability to climb fences. Most Siberians do not scheme to escape their surroundings, however. They dig for the thrill of digging and sometimes keep to their task until a hole large enough for lying down in has been devised.

Note: In some towns, laws have been enacted banning "vicious dogs," which potentially means any free-roaming dog. Check your town's rulings in regard to owning dogs. You will have to be zealous in making sure your dog never roams freely in a heavily populated neighborhood, as the dog will likely be impounded and possibly banned from returning to the home. Fines on owners deemed negligent often start at $100 and double with every incident.

Traveling with Siberians

Siberian Huskies love companionship and do not like staying home alone. They enjoy new situations, sights, and sounds; they do not enjoy solitude.

Traveling by Car

You should familiarize the dog with riding in the car from the time he is a puppy. The dog always should be placed in the back seat. Teach him to lie down or, preferably, to ride in his crate when the car is in motion. If your car is

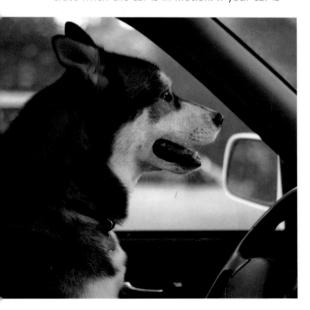

large enough to have open space at the back, you can purchase a dog grille to partition off an area for the dog. This keeps the dog from moving about and encourages him to settle down. There are also dog "safety belts" for use in the back seat that can be purchased from pet stores.

The car windows should be opened approximately 2 inches (5 cm) to improve air circulation during the ride. If you travel frequently without air-conditioning during hot weather, you can purchase specially designed window screens that allow more air to enter the window. When traveling during hot periods, your dog should receive a small amount of water at regular intervals to prevent dehydration. Make it a habit to bring an insulated container of cold water with you wherever you go. There are also two important "nevers."

Never allow the dog to hang his head out the window while the car is in motion. This can result in eye, ear, and throat injuries.

Never leave a dog unattended in a parked car during the heat of the day. The temperature inside a parked car can soar in just minutes and can prove fatal to the dog. Puppies are especially susceptible to heatstroke.

If you are taking a trip of more than one hour, do not feed the dog for approximately four to six hours before leaving, as a full stomach can often lead to motion sickness. Withhold water two hours before the trip. If your dog is highly excitable or prone to vomiting in the car and you are planning an extended ride, consult your veterinarian regarding possible medications. Tranquilizers should be used only when absolutely necessary, when prescribed by the veterinarian, as the primary effect of these drugs is to make the dog drowsy. They don't minimize the dog's physical discomfort and do, in fact, inhibit the dog's ability to regulate body temperature. Most dogs will outgrow a tendency toward motion sickness as they get more accustomed to trips in the car.

On extended trips, stop every two hours or so to let the dog relieve himself, have a drink, and get some exercise. It is especially important to remember to keep a Siberian Husky on leash during such stops.

Special arrangements and advance reservations may need to be made if your trip requires overnight lodging, because many facilities will not allow dogs. Your local automobile club or published travel guides may be able to give you a list of places near your destination that allow animals. You can also search the Internet for a list of pet-friendly hotels in the area.

Bring an adequate supply of the dog's normal food on long trips. This helps reduce the chance of digestive problems. A traveling dog is faced already with many new and unusual conditions; having to switch to a new food is another chance to upset him.

Traveling by Plane

Traveling by airplane used to be a dangerous proposition for animals, as they were treated merely as cargo. In the last decade, however, regulations have been passed that have greatly improved air travel. All animals must now be better protected in flight and shielded from extremes of temperature. Traveling in airplanes has become commonplace for show dogs— many of which compete from coast to coast. Many breeders will have planned matings that involve partners from various areas of the country, making a quick airplane trip a necessity (usually for the bitch).

Every year in the United States more than two million pets and other live animals are transported by air. Federal and state governments impose restrictions on transporting live animals, and each airline establishes its own company policy for animal transport. As a shipper or owner you also have a responsibility to take the necessary precautions to ensure the well being of the animal.

It is imperative to check with the airline you intend to use before finalizing travel arrangements. A licensed veterinarian should examine your Siberian within ten days prior to shipment and issue a certificate stating that the animal is in good health. Airlines may not require health certificates for service animals used by passengers with disabilities.

Passenger Cabin Travel

The Federal Aviation Administration (FAA) allows each airline to decide if they will allow you to travel with your pet inside the passenger cabin. If an airline does allow pets inside the cabin, the pet container is considered to be carry-on baggage and must follow all carry-on baggage rules and restrictions, including:
• Your pet container must be small enough to fit underneath the seat without blocking any person's path to the main aisle of the airplane.
• Your pet container must remain properly stowed the entire time the airplane is moving on the airport surface and for takeoff and landing.
• You must follow flight attendant instructions regarding the proper stowage of your pet container.

These baggage restrictions all but negate the possibility of flying with your Siberian inside the cabin, unless it is a puppy. Some air carriers may impose a special fee or "excess baggage" charge for this service.

In addition, most airlines have policies and procedures in place to make sure that the flight is comfortable for all passengers on the airplane. These additional procedures may include:

• a limited list of the types of pets that you can bring into the cabin;
• a limit on the number of pets in the cabin;
• a limit on the number of pets that may accompany you on the airplane;
• a requirement that your pet be harmless, inoffensive, and odorless;
• a requirement that your pet remain in the container for the entire flight;
• a requirement that you be able to produce a recently issued health certificate for your pet.

Cargo Travel

Pets may be shipped as unaccompanied cargo, and many airline cargo departments employ specialists in the movement of animals. Each airline establishes its own policies, and animals who do not meet the carry-on size requirements must be shipped in pressurized holds.

Federal travel regulations are also derived from the federal Animal Welfare Act, which is enforced by the Animal and Plant Health Inspection Service of the U.S. Department of Agriculture (USDA). They have established several additional important requirements, including the following:

1. Dogs must be at least eight weeks old and must have been weaned for at least five days.

2. Cages and other shipping containers must meet the minimum standard for size, ventila-tion, strength, sanitation, and design for safe handling. (Sky kennels furnished by the airlines meet these requirements.)

3. Dogs must not be brought to the airline for shipping more than four hours before departure. (Six hours is permitted if shipping arrangements are made in advance.)

4. If puppies less than 16 weeks of age are in transit more than 12 hours, food and water must be provided. Older animals must have food at least every 24 hours and water at least every 12 hours. Written instructions for food and water must accompany all animals shipped, regardless of the scheduled time in transit.

5. Animals may not be exposed to tem-peratures less than 45°F (7°C), unless they are accompanied by a certificate signed by a vet-erinarian stating that they are acclimated to lower temperatures.

6. Animals cannot be shipped "Cash On Delivery" (COD) unless the shipper guaran-tees the return freight, should the animals be refused at destination.

Precautions for Plane Travel

Beyond compliance with federal regulations and airline company policy, there are a number of precautions you can take to ensure the wel-fare of your Siberian.

Because the space allotment for animals on an airplane is limited, be sure to make an advance reservation for the dog. Try to sched-ule a nonstop (or at least direct) flight; avoid connections and the heavy traffic of a holiday or weekend flight. There is an added risk of the dog being misplaced or injured if he must be moved around to make connecting flights. If the dog must travel on connecting flights, arrange to break up the long trip with a rest stop. For overseas travel (including Hawaii), inquire about any special health requirements, such as quarantines.

If given proper notice, most airlines are able to furnish owners with suitable crates for shipping their dogs, for an additional charge. Dogs that are already accustomed to spending time in a crate will be less stressed than first-timers. If possible, allow a newcomer to try out the crate a few times before the actual trip. Make sure the door latches securely.

Check with the airline prior to departure for instructions regarding how to board the dog, and where to pick him up once you arrive. To keep upsets to a minimum, the owner should also send a supply of the dog's normal food along on the trip.

Withhold food for eight to ten hours before the flight, and be sure that the dog is exercised just prior to entering the crate. A soiled crate will make the dog very uncomfortable during the flight.

The shipping crate should be marked clearly on the outside with "Live Animal," the dog's name, and the name, address, and phone number of both the sender and recipient. Make sure your dog is wearing a tag with the same information. Tape another copy of this information *to the inside of the crate* with the dog. Also consider having an additional temporary tag with your destination's address and phone number. Bring a current photo of your pet in case he is lost.

You may want to place a blanket or some shredded newspaper at the bottom of the crate for a little added comfort for the dog. Enclose a nylon bone to help alleviate tension and boredom during the trip. Do not place food or water inside the crate before departure, as invariably it will spill and make the trip uncomfortable for the dog. You should, however, try to attach a water dish to the inside of the crate near the bars so that an attendant could pour water for the dog without having to open the crate, should the need arise.

Many novice shippers make the mistake of sedating their dogs before an air flight. Although it is true that a nervous dog can panic and injure himself during flight, it is better to teach the dog to relax in the crate rather than sedate him. Tranquilizers can depress respiration, and this factor—when combined with excessive heat and oxygen reduction, which are common conditions during air flight—can sometimes lead to heatstroke and death. Do not administer sedatives to your Siberian without the prior approval of a veterinarian. If such approval is given, be sure to provide a test dose some time before the trip to see how your pet will react. Verify that your airline allows sedated animals to fly when making your flight arrangements.

Stay with the crate for as long as possible. When you board, try to tell a pilot or a flight attendant that there is a pet in the cargo hold. The airlines have a system for providing these notifications, but it can't hurt to mention it. Notify every airline official connected with your flight that you have a dog being loaded. (I believe in being pesty when dealing with such valuable cargo!) Verify with airline officials that the dog has, indeed, been loaded on the plane before leaving the airport. If there is an extended delay or cancellation of the flight, you will want to be there to make new arrangements for the dog. You cannot be too careful when leaving your Siberian in someone else's care.

Boarding Your Siberian

Occasionally, you will need to find good accommodations for your pet while you are away. Whatever method you use, always leave enough of the dog's normal food to last until your return. The best solution is, of course, to have someone the dog is familiar with take care of him. If this is impossible, ask the breeder from whom you purchased the dog to temporarily board him. The advantages of this are the familiarity he would have with the individual dog and the particular requirements and traits of Siberians. Because this breed needs a lot of human companionship, this may be a very beneficial arrangement for all concerned.

Boarding also is available at the facilities of some veterinarians or at commercial kennels. These establishments are usually well managed, clean, and attentive to the dog's basic needs. Be sure to visit and inspect the kennel beforehand. Ask about the daily exercise routines and feeding procedures and check that it is accredited by the Pet Care Services Association (PCSA). You can expect to pay from $30 to $50 per day for this service. You can obtain a list of approved kennels in your area by writing the PCSA (see page 92 for the address).

Many Siberian owners prefer to hire a professional "pet sitter" to come into their home several times a day to walk and feed their dog. This service is less disruptive for the pet than boarding. A list of accredited pet sitters can be obtained from Pet Sitters International at *www.petsit.com.*

Protecting Your Siberian

A sad side effect of the breed's popularity has been an increased number of Siberian Husky thefts. Several animal protection agencies have issued a warning that dognapping is on the increase. It may seem hard to imagine that a stranger would attempt to steal a Siberian Husky from his home or yard, but it does happen. Some dogs are more affable than others, and professional thieves often employ elaborate methods to restrain or entice a dog (such as parading a bitch in heat near an eager male). You can help protect your dog—and your neighborhood—by never leaving him unattended outside the home.

Although many owners believe that a tag on the dog's collar listing his name and the owner's name, address, and phone number will suffice in helping the dog find his way home should he somehow stray, this protection is limited. The collar could be torn off by the dog or purposely removed by a thief. There are two more reliable sources to identify and find your missing dog: microchip implantation and tattooing.

Microchips

This high-tech method of identification has become quite popular. A tiny microchip containing information on the dog and his medical history is injected just under the skin at the base of the dog's neck. The injection procedure is painless for the animal and the chip is embedded permanently. A hand-held scanner placed over the chip will retrieve the microchip's information, which then can be decoded by a computer at the central registry that records the specific information on the dog. Most humane society shelters and veterinarians now have scanners, which are being used to identify a higher percentage of lost animals each year and return them

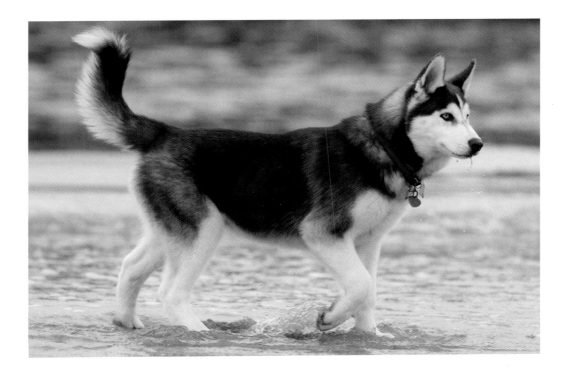

to their owners. The procedure is relatively inexpensive, and there is a nominal annual renewal fee to keep the dog's information on file in the national registry. In addition, many animal shelters and non-profit animal groups sponsor low-cost microchipping services.

Tattooing

It is also a good idea to have your Siberian Husky tattooed. This relatively painless procedure can be performed by most veterinarians for a nominal fee. Many dog clubs also hold annual clinics to perform this service for dog owners. The use of tattoos is endorsed by dog organizations, and show competitors are not penalized for having a tattoo.

The tattoo will be a permanent aid for identifying the dog should he become lost. It also will prevent the dog from being sold to research laboratories that sometimes purchase strays.

In most cases, the dog's AKC registration number or the owner's social security number is tattooed onto the dog's inner thigh. Although the inside of the ear can also be used, there have been cases where a dog's ear has been cut off to remove the tattoo. The tattoo number should then be listed with one of the national registries, which will record (for an annual fee) all pertinent information.

FEEDING SIBERIAN HUSKIES

What you feed your dog will have a direct impact on his overall health and longevity.

Make sure to select a food that is complete nutritionally, and is balanced to suit your dog's particular lifestyle. Most popular brands available in the local supermarket or from pet shops and suppliers are the end result of many years of research into canine nutrition. An owner should still do a bit of comparative shopping and label reading before deciding on a brand, as the most popular dog food may not be the best food for your Siberian Husky.

Types of Food

What type of food is best for your Siberian Husky? There are several possible answers. Some owners use only one type, whereas others use a combination. The task is to present a daily ration that is nutritionally complete and balanced and suited to your dog's particular lifestyle. Which type of food is best? Which brand is best? The owner must consider many

factors and then do some comparative shopping when making this decision.

Dry Food

Ounce for ounce, dry food is the least expensive type, and, accordingly, is the most commonly used. There can be great variation in the quality of dry foods, however. Dry foods are composed of 8 to 10 percent water, with the remaining ingredients being various cereals, soy, meat by-products, and small amounts of fats, vitamins, and minerals.

Buy only those brands labeled "nutritionally complete;" however, keep in mind that this label is not the only determining factor you should check. Some dry products require the dog to eat an excessive amount of the food to fulfill daily dietary needs. Various products' intake requirements can be determined by examining the suggested feeding amounts per weight of dog as listed on the package. A dry

CHECKLIST

Rules for Feeding

The following basic rules may help protect your Siberian Husky from feeding-related problems.

✔ Supply ample amounts of clean, fresh water at all times, especially in hot weather.

✔ Wash all food and water bowls daily in hot, soapy water to prevent bacterial growth.

✔ Maintain a constant diet, as sudden changes may cause digestive upset.

✔ Introduce new foods slowly, in modest amounts mixed in with the food the dog is accustomed to.

✔ Bring an ample supply of the dog's usual food when traveling or when the dog must be kenneled.

✔ Take up the water bowl at night if the dog is having problems with housebreaking.

✔ Serve leftover canned food at room temperature.

food that is priced low may, in the long run, be more expensive than other brands because the dog needs to eat more of it to obtain all the benefits from the food. Also, when large amounts of food must be ingested, there will be an inevitable increase in excreted waste materials. A slight variation of content may be observed from batch to batch in many dry food products, as fluctuations in the availability of the base crop (soy, corn, barley) produce a slightly different blending at various times during the year.

The meat-meal based dry foods used by most commercial breeders and sold in pet shops and supply houses offer a stable mixture from batch to batch that nutritionally is complete, easily digested, and contains enough fiber to help produce a firm stool. In addition, the feeding amounts needed to fulfill all nutritional requirements do not force the dog to overeat. These products may cost a bit more on a per pound basis, but the superior quality is worth the added expense.

Many dry food products are low in fat content and may be insufficient for an active dog, such as the Siberian Husky. This easily is compensated for by adding approximately one-half can of canned food or several tablespoons of cottage cheese to the kibble as a supplement. Typically, good-quality adult dog food should be 22 to 25 percent protein and 15 to 19 percent fat. Research has shown that 21 to 24 percent protein is optimum for your dog's various life stages.

However, many pet food companies add low-quality protein products like meat and bone meal, by-products, and corn gluten meal to increase the percentage of crude protein on the label. Low-quality proteins are not easily digestible and may cause digestive issues for the dog. Quality dog foods usually contain more calories per pound and are easier to digest than generic brands, so it takes a smaller quantity of a quality food to meet your Siberian's needs.

Canned Food

Ounce for ounce, canned dog food is very expensive, considering most contain more than 75 percent water. The remaining portion is composed of meat by-products, soy fillers, vitamins, minerals, and, frequently, artificial coloring and preservatives. The high water level and additives often have a diuretic effect on many dogs, resulting in housetraining problems.

The canned food products designed for the various stages of life are most recommended. Canned food should comprise no more than one quarter of the daily intake and should be combined with a high-quality dry food for best results. Few dogs dislike canned food, so this is a recommended food for dogs needing to gain or maintain weight. Conversely, it is the food to withhold first for overweight dogs.

Semimoist Food

Semimoist foods are usually packaged in pouches or shaped like hamburgers. They are composed primarily of soy meal, meat by-products, and cereal, and contain approximately 25 percent water. This food is very expensive and contains a considerable amount of additives and preservatives. Although the levels of sugar and salt have decreased recently, semimoist products are still very high in calories. Some dogs have had allergic reactions to the preservatives contained in the highly processed semimoist food. This allergy can range from hyperactivity to skin biting or scratching in sensitive dogs.

Home Cooked Meals

If you want to raise a dog strictly on home prepared meals, it is advisable that you do so under the supervision of a veterinarian or nutritionist. You are competing against the products of pet food companies that have

spent millions of dollars specifically on canine nutrition research. Most pet households are well served by commercial products. However, a breeder knows best the needs of his or her dogs. Siberian Huskies used in sled dog racing certainly would need a specialized diet containing high levels of protein for energy and fats to stave off the effects of continued exposure to cold weather, but this supplementation is done in specific amounts at specific times, using their own blend of kibble, meat, and supplements—being sure the end result is nutritionally complete. Similarly, senior Siberians and dogs with specific health problems (such as kidney disease) will need to alter food intake to address these needs.

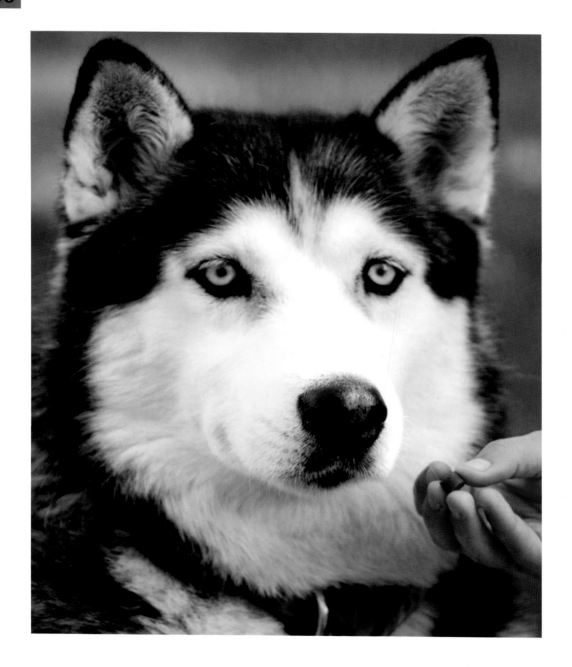

Interested fanciers and homes with more than one Siberian Husky might save some money by devising an individual blend of kibble, meat, vegetables, and cottage cheese. Although this may be effective for lowering the monthly food expense, the primary concern should be nutrition, not saving pennies.

Raw Foods

Dogs of many breeds are susceptible to bloat and torsion, so the less stress on the gastrointestinal tract, the better for your pet. Highly digestible diets are a necessity for Siberians, and some owners recommend feeding a raw food diet—the BARF plan (an acronym for "Bones and Raw Food" or, according to some, "Biologically Appropriate Raw Food").

The BARF diet is based on the premise that when animals are fed a natural, whole food diet, they will be healthier than if fed cooked and processed foods. This philosophy harkens back to the "primal" state for wild canines and is based on human-grade whole foods including raw meat (lamb, chicken, and beef), finely ground bones, offal (entrails and internal organs), and select fruits and vegetables. No grain products are included.

Such a diet should only been undertaken after careful research and with consultation with your veterinarian or nutritionist for guidelines on all dietary requirements.

Supplements

Table scraps can be too much of a good thing for your dog. Although Siberians undoubtedly will love those fatty meat scraps, the end result may be a case of diarrhea. Small amounts of appropriate fruits, vegetables, and cereals will, in fact, promote proper digestion. Be careful, as some fruits and vegetables are harmful to dogs and can even be toxic. These foods include garlic, grapes, raisins, eggplant, avocado, onions, and most nuts. In addition, all forms of the cacao plant (chocolate, cocoa, etc.) should NEVER be fed to your dog, as it contains theobromine—a chemical that can cause upset stomach, vomiting, diarrhea, trembling, and even death. If you are in doubt as to whether a food is suitable for your Siberian, check with your veterinarian or err on the side of caution. Hard or crunchy foods, such as carrots or a sturdy knucklebone, can keep the teeth clean by scraping away tartar along the tooth surface.

Be very selective with bones, however, as these can be constipating and potentially deadly should an improper bone splinter when chewed. Sturdy nylon bones are safest and can be purchased in pet shops, supermarkets, and specialty stores. Although dogs certainly love rawhide bones, they have been linked to intestinal blockage in some dogs, so these should be given sparingly and while the dog is under surveillance. Remove any unfinished portions when you are not around to monitor the dog. **Never** give your Siberian chicken bones!

Aside from nursing mothers, few Siberian Huskies will need vitamin supplements. Vitamin deficiencies are rare and should not occur if a dog is healthy and eating a quality diet. It especially is important not to oversupplement growing puppies, because there can be serious side effects from excessive vitamin intake. A well-balanced diet and an adequate amount of exercise should be all your Siberian Husky needs to stay in good health.

The Feeding Process

Siberian Huskies are eager eaters. They usually clean their bowls quickly and, if satisfied, move off in search of adventure. Few Siberians would put eating ahead of play, if given the chance, so feeding must be supervised and regulated. Wise owners must find the blend that works best for their dog.

Where to Feed

All dogs have pack instincts, and they should be allowed adequate time and space to eat their meal in an out-of-the-way place, rather than in the middle of the kitchen at the busiest time of day. If left to eat in a high-traffic area, a dog may worry whether his food is going to be taken away, and he may develop some bad habits in response. An anxious dog may quickly devour his food. This could lead to digestive problems or vomiting. In the worst case, a dog that gulps his food can develop

a digestive condition called bloat, where the stomach swells after filling with gas and fluids, often twisting and becoming an immediate life-threatening situation.

An anxious dog might also become overprotective of his food. This habit cannot be tolerated, as your Siberian must be trained from an early age to allow you to pick up and remove his food, if necessary, without protest. Occasionally moving the bowl to various places in a room will keep the dog from getting too routinized and will promote healthy eating patterns.

When to Feed

The owner's daily routine and the age of the dog are the main factors in deciding when to feed the dog each day. Puppies need several small meals a day, because they cannot physically handle large amounts of food. If possible, puppies should be allowed to eat when hungry, in a free choice system. This situation is often impossible in a multidog household, as the older dogs will certainly clear any leftovers, in which case three meals usually will suffice. At approximately nine months of age, only two daily meals will be necessary. The adult feeding pattern usually consists of either one large meal a day, generally in the late afternoon or at night, or two smaller meals daily.

How Much to Feed

No definite formula exists for determining how much food one dog will need daily. The dog's appetite will be the natural guide. The amount listed on the label is a guide—every dog has a different metabolism and lifestyle.

Keep in mind, however, that the Siberian is a primal breed, and some dogs may eat in excess.

The breed is not a perfect candidate for free-choice feeding, as some may eat everything that is available to them, regardless of hunger.

Working Siberian Huskies require more calories each day than an older, less active dog. Growing puppies and pregnant or lactating bitches will need a special diet high in protein and calories. Dogs that spend a good deal of time outside during cold weather will require extra calories, usually in the form of supplementary fats, to help them cope with the weather.

Keep the feeding process simple. The dog should have some privacy and ample time to eat his meal (generally 10 to 20 minutes). Pick up and discard any food that remains after this time. You should adjust the amount slightly at the next meal if the dog has been leaving food uneaten, until the dog clears his bowl. If the bowl is quickly emptied, increase the amount slightly until the dog is satisfied. You may also try adding nutritious vegetables like green beans to help your dog feel more full.

Vomiting up a meal can be a problem for Siberians that have a tendency to gulp their food. Along with the food, the dog is taking in too much air into the stomach, which causes the dog to suddenly regurgitate. If this occurs frequently, you should consider serving several small meals each day rather than one or two large ones, thereby limiting the amount of food-and air-in the stomach at any one time. The dog may outgrow this tendency.

Problem Eaters

Should the dog refuse his food, discard what remains and do not offer a replacement until the next scheduled meal. By catering to the

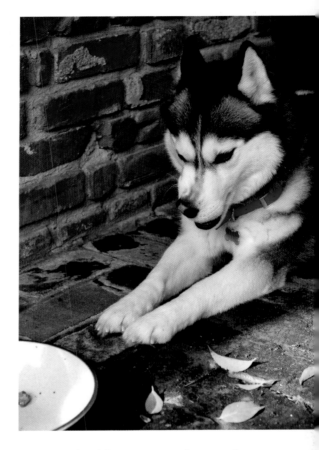

demands of a picky eater you enhance, rather than solve, the problem. If the dog appears hungry and healthy and still continues to turn away from his food, change what you are feeding him *one time* and see if the dog only had an aversion to the food you have been giving. Some dog food companies change the contents of their product slightly from batch to batch, so the dog may dislike the current batch. However, Siberian Huskies rarely are problem eaters. A sudden lack of interest in eating usually is caused by a health or behavioral problem. If the problem persists for more than a few meals, the dog should be examined by a veterinarian.

If there is no physical reason for this lack of appetite, chalk it up to stubbornness. Few dogs will continue this for long once they see that you will not give in. Never whine or plead with the dog to eat. You will either convince the dog that there really is something wrong with the food (why else would my master be carrying on about it?) or he will sense your insecurity and exploit it.

Teething and Chewing

A Siberian Husky will chew while teething, so owners should be aware and prepare for it. A puppy has a strong urge to chew between four and ten months of age, but don't be fooled into thinking it will all end in a few months. The need to chew will remain as the dog matures.

The best method to rid accumulated tartar buildup on the teeth (short of a professional scraping or ultrasonic cleaning) is by chewing hard substances. Because there is little of this in the diet, other objects must be found. Some dogs also chew to release tension, often causing extensive and expensive damage to household goods. A Siberian Husky left alone for long stretches would be a prime candidate.

No simple, foolproof method exists to stop dogs from chewing. Each Siberian will come up with his own "hit list." The best course is prevention. Give the dog an ample supply of suitable chew objects, and let him know exactly what *may* and *may not* be chewed. Do not give the dog an old slipper as a chew toy and then expect him to leave the rest of your shoes alone. Although most dogs enjoy rawhide bones, Siberian Huskies usually can devour them quickly, and rawhide has been linked to intestinal blockage. Nylon bones are long lasting and sturdy, but many dogs don't like them. Hard beef or veal bones, such as from the knuckle, should be given only occasionally, as they can be constipating and abrasive to tooth enamel. Plastic toys and stuffed playthings should only be given when the dog is being supervised, as these can be torn apart and swallowed, leading to choking.

While the dog is teething he will need to chew. To keep losses to a minimum, confine the

Chewing Away Tartar

• If you routinely give your Siberian some hard or crunchy food, such as carrots or a sturdy knucklebone, the chewing will naturally scrape away the tartar that accumulates along the surface of the teeth and at the gum line. This, plus routine brushing, can help avoid having to get your dog's teeth professionally cleaned.

• Choose bones carefully because a low-quality bone can splinter when chewed. Nylon or rawhide bones are the safest choice among the commercial products. Check where the product is made, however, as many are imported from countries that do not carefully monitor pet products.

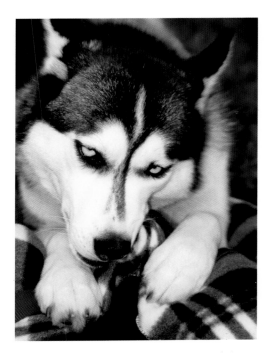

dog when he cannot be supervised and always have a suitable chew toy available. The need to chew will continue even after the first teeth are shed. There may be another intense bout with chewing when the back molars are emerging at around eight or nine months of age.

Unfortunately, learning to deal with teething is a trial-and-error process. If you give your dog access to all areas of your house, you may discover that your Siberian Husky has developed a taste for your book collection or venetian blinds. If you catch the dog with a forbidden object in his mouth, immediately remove it from the dog's clutches, shake it in front of the dog's head and tap it as you say *"No!"* in a stern voice. This will help the dog to connect your displeasure with its chewing of the object.

If the dog continues chewing, add a quick but nonviolent shake of the neck to your correction. This is intended to shock the dog, not injure him. Replace the forbidden object with something that the dog is allowed to chew.

Chewing can be fatal for the dog should he ever bite on an electric cord. An inquisitive puppy often will mouth wires, so be sure to secure them during your puppy-proofing of the household. Many plants are poisonous if ingested, and dogs often are attracted to them by their smell or appearance. If you have poisonous plants in the household (such as poinsettia, dieffenbachia, or foxglove), place them out of the puppy's reach. A list of toxic plants is available online, or you can ask your veterinarian.

GROOMING SIBERIAN HUSKIES

Siberians have double coats that insulate against extreme weather conditions.

Coat Care

The Siberian Husky is a double-coated breed. This means that it has a woolly undercoat that serves as the dog's insulation against cold or heat, and a layer of longer, harsher outercoat that grows through the undercoat. Shedding will occur at least once a year in males and twice a year (generally spring and fall) in females. High humidity or excessive heat often will make the shedding worse. Because the amount of hair shed by a Siberian is substantial, this should be kept in mind when deciding to purchase this breed.

The shedding process usually will take from three to six weeks, with a new coat growing in during the next three to four months. During the active shedding period, groom the dog daily. Between shedding times, regular brushing will remove excess loose hairs. If you maintain a weekly grooming pattern, you should not be plagued continually by hair left behind wherever the dog has been, as is common with some other long-haired breeds.

The main goal of grooming is to remove dead hairs that are clinging to the coat. In the process, you are also cleaning the skin and the shafts of the living hair.

The Siberian's coat is not to be shaved, cut, or trimmed. When they are shaved, they are more susceptible to skin allergies, sunburns, and parasite infestations. Very minor tidying of stray hairs may occur in show dogs, but shaping or stripping of the Siberian's coat is unwarranted. One exception to this rule concerns the Siberian's feet, which have hairs on the bottom of the paw and in between the toes that grow continuously. These tufts of hair should be trimmed short regularly, as these hairs can collect mud and debris as well as painful balls of ice in the winter.

Grooming Tools

Basic grooming tools are inexpensive and paramount in importance for the maintenance of your dog's coat. The main tools for grooming the Siberian Husky are a shedding blade, a wide-toothed comb, and a bristle brush.

The shedding blade is a bent, U-shaped piece of metal that is held together by a handle. One side of the blade has small, dulled teeth that catch and remove excess hair from the coat. Use this tool first, before proceeding with the wide-toothed comb. The tips of the comb's teeth must always be rounded, and the bristles of the brush must be long enough to reach through the coat to the skin.

The comb should be used to run through the coat to break up any mats or snags and to remove the dead hairs. Knots should be worked out a little at a time, using the comb and the fingers to gently tease the hairs apart. It is especially important to comb through the undercoat during shedding. A fine-toothed comb is handy for the areas under the chin and tail and between the ears. Use the brush once the combing is complete to finish off the coat. Brush the coat forward, over the head and shoulders, before combing it back. Brush the rear areas in the direction of the lay of the coat. Extra attention should be given to the hindquarters, as guard hairs in this area often accumulate into mats.

Because Siberians are susceptible to skin allergies, be sure to have a veterinarian check the coat if you notice any excessive scratching or biting at the skin.

Bathing

The Siberian Husky will not need bathing more than twice a year, usually in the spring and fall, coinciding with the molting of the coat. The Siberian's coat remains clean year-round and should not take on a "doggy" odor.

When bathing is needed, use a very mild soap designed especially for dogs—not products for humans, because they are too harsh and drying for a dog's hair. Wet the dog thoroughly, working the water down through the undercoat to the skin. Begin with the head and proceed down, being very careful that water and shampoo do not get into the dog's eyes and ears. Once the dog is lathered fully, rinse the coat well with lots of warm water. The soap must be totally removed from the undercoat or else the skin may become irritated, and the dog may develop dandruff or experience skin irritation.

Towel the dog down, and do not expose him to any cool air until the undercoat is dried totally. A hair dryer set on low may be used to speed the drying process. Once dry, give the dog a complete grooming to be sure that no mats or knots have formed.

Nail Care

Although most Siberians get enough exposure to rough pavement to keep their nails naturally worn down, owners still should inspect the nails regularly to ensure that they do not need to be trimmed. Overgrown nails can impede the normal placement of the foot and affect a dog's gait.

Most dogs naturally are reluctant to have their feet held for any time. To counteract this instinct to pull away, regularly touch and play with his feet and toes while petting and grooming to indoctrinate the puppy to having this area touched. You can later try massaging the footpads. This will prepare the dog should the nails ever need a clipping.

A specially designed guillotine clipper, which can be purchased from pet stores, grooming shops, and veterinarians, should be used to trim the nails. If you are inexperienced, have your veterinarian show you this simple procedure. Once you are instructed, this process can often be handled at home. For dogs that find this stressful and struggle when you try to secure the paw, however, professional help will be required.

Cut only the outer shell of the nail, as cutting too close to the vein (called the "quick") is quite painful for the dog and can cause bleeding. Once shortened to its proper length, smooth the surface of the nail with a few brushes of an emery board. If you cut too close to the quick and the nail bleeds, apply pressure to the area by holding a piece of cotton gauze over the nail or use a styptic pencil. Once the bleeding stops, dab the nail with a mild antiseptic.

For owners (and dogs) who are not comfortable with nail trimming, many veterinarians and groomers offer nail grinding services. This handheld, rotating device sands down the nail cuticle, essentially eliminating the danger of cutting into the quick. One drawback is that your Siberian may not like the noise and continued pressure that is required to grind the nail.

Foot Care

The pads of the feet should be inspected regularly, especially if the dog limps or favors a leg. Burrs, splinters, or stones can become embedded in and between the pads of the foot, and scratches and cuts on the pad are common. For minor problems, a gentle cleaning, using sterilized tweezers to remove any objects and a mild antiseptic, should work effectively.

If the dog suddenly acquires a limp and favors or licks one foot, he may have been stung by an insect. If this is the case, apply an ice compress to reduce or prevent swelling and ease the pain. Unless there is an allergic reaction of some sort (see Stinging Insects, page 69), this discomfort should pass quickly.

If there is no evidence of a cut or sting, and the dog still indicates pain in the foot, there may be an injury to the bones or muscle tissue, or there may be an object deeply embedded in the footpad. Although rarely serious, these conditions require the expertise of a veterinarian.

During the winter, your Siberian's feet may be exposed to chemicals that are placed on the sidewalks to melt ice and snow. These compounds can be caustic to a dog's footpads and skin. If the dog has walked on these chemicals, rinse his feet with warm, soapy water. If the dog's pads appear sensitive to the touch, apply a thin layer of petroleum jelly to soothe them. If these chemicals are not removed, the dog may try to alleviate the discomfort by licking them. Ingesting such poisonous materials can be hazardous to the dog's digestive tract and overall health.

HOW–TO: HEALTH CHECK

Evaluating Your Dog's Condition

A quick inspection of your dog performed during his routine grooming sessions is a good way to observe his overall health. Start by running your hands over the dog's entire body and feeling for anything unusual, such as cuts, swelling, cysts, or areas that cause the dog pain when touched. Be sure to get your fingers through the double coat and down to the skin to look and feel for signs of irritation. You should then turn to the head and begin a more thorough evaluation.

Eyes

A slight discharge in the corner of the eyes is normal and can be cleared easily with a damp, lint-free cloth. Do not use cotton balls because they can leave tiny fibers in the eye. A clear discharge usually is related to tear drainage or minor irritations and inflammations, such as conjunctivitis. Consult your veterinarian if this discharge becomes excessive or changes to a cloudy or yellowish color, or if the dog blinks constantly and the eye is red.

A Siberian Husky may get a minor scratch on the eye when running through the underbrush. This should heal quickly without any special attention. If a burr or small object gets into the eye, irrigate the eye with some warm water or saline solution and carefully dab the corner with a soft cloth. If it becomes lodged, seek immediate veterinary care, as probing for it may injure the eye. A constant discharge or a pawing of the area requires a veterinary inspection.

Ears

A dog with ear problems constantly will shake his head or rub his ears with his paws or on the ground. If there is an excessive amount of visible earwax, redness, swelling, or a foul odor coming from the ear canal, a veterinarian's attention is required.

Simple abrasions are the most common ear irritation. Keep the afflicted area clean to avoid infection.

Never probe down into the dog's ear canal or use a cotton swab (Q-tip), as this can be extremely painful and can cause great damage. To help remove the normal accumulation of wax and dirt in the outer ear, swab the easily accessible areas of the ear with a cotton ball wet with a little warm water. Ear cleaning solutions can also be purchased at pet stores. Ointments made specially for cleaning the ear can be purchased from pet stores, groomers, or your veterinarian if cleanliness is a continual problem. Avoid oily compounds because they may attract and retain dirt.

If you suspect that the inner ear is clogged with wax or he winces with pain when his ears are touched, seek veterinary care. An inflammation of the ear, termed otitis, will need to be treated topically or systemically, depending on the causative agent.

Tooth Care

Tartar can be a lifelong problem for dogs. A diet that includes items naturally abrasive to the teeth (such as carrots) can help keep teeth clean. Chewing a safe, hard bone will remove most buildup, as will dental bones.

Accustoming your Siberian from puppyhood to having his teeth gently cleaned with a specialized fingertip brush, a soft child's toothbrush or moistened gauze pad will ease your task in later years when the teeth require more cleaning. Proper pet toothbrushes will never have bristles that reach under the gum line. A yellowing of the tooth exterior is common as the dog ages and often can be minimized by routine treatment. The teeth can be brushed once or twice a week with a flavored dog toothpaste (available at pet stores) or a mild paste of baking soda and hydrogen peroxide to remove most stains and plaque.

Note: Human toothpaste contains detergent chemicals and should **not** be used for pets, as they will swallow the paste.

The proper brushing technique is to place the toothbrush bristles at a 45-degree angle, aimed where the gum and teeth meet. Gently move the bristles in an oval pattern, covering three to four teeth at a time. Complete ten short rotations before moving to a new area in the mouth. The upper "canine" teeth do the most chewing and should get the most attention.

For best results, brushing should begin when your pet is young. As dogs age and develop tooth and gum sensitivities, there may be pain associated with brushing, and they may be less willing to allow it.

If discoloring remains despite weekly brushings, the teeth may need to be scaled by your veterinarian. If the buildup is chronic, your veterinarian can show you how to perform this scaling at home as part of the dog's regular grooming process.

A sudden change in the dog's breath that lasts for more than a few days may indicate a problem with either the teeth or the throat, as well as internal problems like kidney disease and organ damage. A loss of appetite could stem from decayed teeth, which make it painful for the dog to eat. Inspect the teeth and gums for any obvious sign of infection, swell-

ing, bleeding, or sensitivity to the touch. An abscessed tooth sometimes manifests itself as a boil-like growth on the cheek area. Your veterinarian should be informed as soon as you notice any of these conditions.

Periodontal Diseases

Periodontal (gum) diseases, including gingivitis and periodontitis, are serious infections that—if left untreated—can lead to tooth loss and internal health issues. Periodontal disease is one of the most common and serious pet health problems, affecting nearly 80% of all dogs by age three. At-home prevention is as important as regular teeth cleaning by veterinarians to combat this threat.

Periodontal disease often results in tooth and gum infections, severe pain, loss of teeth, and even organ damage, which occurs when bacteria from the infected areas gain access to the bloodstream (a condition called bacteremia). Prevention is the key to managing gum disease. If the surfaces of the teeth are cleaned frequently, the gums will stay healthy.

SAFEGUARDING YOUR DOG'S HEALTH

Preventive health care begins in puppyhood and continues throughout your Siberian's life.

Veterinary Care

Regardless of your Siberian Husky's outward condition, he should get an annual physical examination from your veterinarian. At this time, he or she will evaluate the dog's general condition, test for internal parasites, and determine if the dog needs any injections.

Any dog that shows symptoms of illness, weight loss, or abnormal behavior (such as drinking excessive amounts of water) should be taken to a veterinarian shortly after noticing the problem. Delaying treatment can be a costly mistake. Many illnesses that are treated easily in the early stages can become life-threatening if treatment is delayed.

Basic Health Care

There are several simple procedures that every pet owner should know and some that are best left to health care professionals.

Taking the Temperature

The first is taking a dog's temperature. Lubricate the end of a heavy-duty rectal thermometer with a little petroleum or KY jelly. As a safety precaution, you may want to have an assistant help restrain the dog during the insertion so that the dog does not inadvertently sit down or otherwise break the thermometer. It is best to have the dog stand, but he can also lie on his side. One person should get a secure grasp on the dog while the other lifts the tail and inserts the thermometer. To get an accurate reading, the thermometer should remain inserted for one to two minutes. A dog's normal temperature is slightly higher than a human's—100 to 102°F (37.7–38.9°C) is normal.

Signs of Heatstroke

With a long-haired, thick-coated dog such as the Siberian Husky, owners must be vigilant to make sure their pet maintains a healthy temperature. Prevent heat exhaustion by taking care not to overexert or overexercise your pet on hot days, making sure there is access to water, and retreating to air conditioned areas when signs of overheating first occur. During the warm months, it is a good idea to carry cold water and a portable bowl on outings.

A dog's normal breathing uses most of his lung capacity and is approximately 35 breaths per minute. If the dog begins to get too hot, the breathing increases to panting. Signs of heat exhaustion include heavy panting, hyperventilation (deep, quickened breathing), wide eyes with a glassy appearance, increased salivation followed by dry gums, weakness, confusion or inattention, vomiting or diarrhea, and occasionally bleeding. As the condition progresses toward heat prostration/heatstroke, there may be paleness or graying to the gums, a shallowing of breath, vomiting, diarrhea, and, finally, seizures or a comatose state.

Temperatures above 105°F (41°C) are considered dangerous and warrant immediate medical attention. Even in dogs that recover from heatstroke, there is sometimes irreversible organ damage, causing lifelong health problems. In addition, dogs that have overheated once are more susceptible to overheating again in the future.

Never leave your Siberian alone in the car during the hot summer months, even if the windows are cracked. Temperatures inside parked cars can reach lethal temperatures in minutes.

Giving Medication

Most dog owners will have to give their pet medication at one time or another. Although giving a dog a pill or capsule may seem like a simple enough procedure, most dogs quickly master the technique for not swallowing pills and defiantly spitting them right out. The easiest method is to disguise the pill in something tasty, such as a small chunk of liverwurst or hamburger, or wrapped in a piece of cheese. If your dog is not so easily tricked, gently pry the dog's mouth open by applying pressure at the back of his mouth, tilt the head up *slightly,* and insert the pill as far back on the tongue as possible. Close the jaws and watch for a swallow. Gently stroking the throat may help. *Never lift the dog's head straight up and drop in the pill; in this position, the pill can be inhaled into the windpipe rather than swallowed.*

The best way to administer liquid medicine is to place it in a medicine spoon or syringe and pour it into the *back of the mouth* by lifting up the side of the dog's lower lip by the back molars and holding the head *slightly* upward. This method lets the medicine slide down the throat. Keep a grasp around the dog's muzzle until you are sure it has swallowed or else the dog may easily spit the medicine out. Again, never hold the head in an exaggerated upward position, as this invites choking.

Although some liquid and powdered medicines may be mixed into the dog's food (check with your veterinarian first), many dogs smell or taste the additives right away and won't eat the food. If this is the case, powdered medications usually can be liquefied by adding a little water, and you can proceed as described above.

Monitoring the Heart

A dog's heartbeat also can be monitored easily. Although a Siberian Husky's normal heartbeat is 60 to 90 beats per minute, it may vary because of factors such as age, temperature, exertion, stress, and illness. A pulse can be found in the front paw, but the one located on the inside of the thigh is the easiest to take. Press softly against the pulse and monitor the pattern and rate of the beats. This procedure should be performed if you ever notice signs of extreme fatigue, fainting, or hyperactivity in your dog. Any abnormal patterns in the heartbeat require immediate attention by a veterinarian.

Monitoring Breathing

You should also be aware of your dog's normal rate of breathing. When relaxed, the breathing should be easy and smooth—from 10 to 30 breaths per minute.

Vaccinations

Most puppies receive their first immunizations while still with their breeder. These initial vaccinations are for distemper, hepatitis, and parvovirus at around six to eight weeks. Follow-up shots will be required for most vaccines, on a schedule devised by your veterinarian (generally every three weeks until the initial boosters are finished). A rabies vaccination also will be needed, as well as boosters as the dog matures. By keeping the required vaccinations and boosters current, you can protect your dog from many infectious diseases. Get the records of your dog's earliest shots from the breeder and give this information to your veterinarian. Ask the breeder if the dog has been tested or treated for worms. If it has, find out what type of worm the dog was infected with, what medication was used to treat it, and how the dog reacted to the medication. Worms

are very common in puppies, and this background information can be very helpful.

Leptospirosis

Leptospira is a spirochete bacteria with more than 250 different subtypes ("serovars"), and it is communicable to humans. Since 1983, there has been an increased prevalence of Leptospira disease—also known as leptospirosis—largely due to the urbanization of rural areas, which has increased contact between dogs and wildlife.

Leptospira generally targets adult animals one to six years old, but all ages and breeds can be affected. Dogs who are most commonly infected are those who are often outdoors, have a high exposure to surface water, and weigh more than 15 pounds. If a house or apartment has a problem with mice or rats, dogs and humans that live there are at a higher risk of exposure.

The incubation period varies between three and 20 days; the early signs of disease include lethargy, vomiting, and fever. Other symptoms include weight loss, increased drinking and urinating, diarrhea, abdominal/lumbar pain, jaundice, stiffness/reluctance to walk, enlarged kidneys, and low platelet count (thrombocytopenia).

Vaccination of dogs for leptospirosis has been controversial in recent years. Early vaccines protected against strains *bratislava* and *canicola*. However, there is no cross-protection between the various subtypes in vaccines. It was also suspected that older leptospira vaccines caused a large number of adverse reactions. It has since been determined that it was the contaminants in the vaccine, and not the leptospira, that caused the adverse reaction. Some Siberian experts believe in avoiding the vaccine, while others are proponents. Regardless, if you feel uncomfortable about the vaccine, speak to your veterinarian about whether he or she thinks it is necessary for your pet.

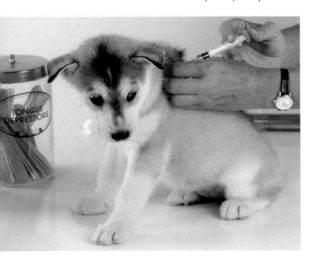

Parasites

Outdoor-loving dogs such as Siberian Huskies are often in contact with contaminations that can produce parasite infections. Owners should closely watch the dog's condition so that problems can be caught early. This vigilance is especially important in the warm months, when infestations are more prevalent.

Worms

Although worms are very common in dogs (especially puppies), they should never be ignored. Severe worm infestations can be very debilitating and sometimes life-threatening. Diagnosing the type of worm and selecting the proper medication is a job only for a veterinarian. Routine wormings using over-the-counter preparations are unnecessary and can be dangerous.

Symptoms of worm infestation include weight loss, weakness, a bloated stomach, diarrhea, dull coat, foul breath, raspy cough, loss of appetite, or, alternatively, a voracious appetite. The dog may drag his anus across the ground or lick and bite around the tail area. In some cases, segments of worms may cling to the dog's feces and be visible on cleanup. Some infected dogs will give little outward sign of the problem until heavily infested, which highlights the importance of having the dog routinely checked for worms.

Detecting the presence of most worms is done by microscopic examination of stool or blood samples. The most common types of worm are the roundworm, tapeworm, hookworm, and heartworm. Each requires a specific medicine. In the case of heartworm (a disease primarily spread by mosquitoes), once the dog has been shown by blood test to be free of the parasite, a *preventive* medication in the form of a pill or chew treat can be administered on a monthly basis throughout mosquito season (early spring until after a killing frost) to keep the dog free from infection. In warm climates, the drug should be given year-round.

Many owners prefer to keep the dog on this medication year-round, as this will avoid having to have the dog's blood tested again at the start of the next mosquito season. This will also decrease the chance of your Siberian contracting this grave disease, which kills thousands of dogs each year. It takes up to six months for heartworms to be detectable. Early signs of infection may include coughing, especially after physical activity, and difficulty breathing. Heartworm infestations may cause seizures, lethargy, weakness, and lack of appetite. Treatment varies with the size and number of adult heartworms in the heart and major vessels, and it may require surgical intervention. There are also pills available that combine heartworm protection with medication that will prevent flea infestation by breaking the flea life cycle at the egg stage (see below).

Fleas

Fleas can make a dog's life miserable. They invade the host, bite his skin, suck his blood, itch unbearably, and sometimes infect the dog with tapeworm. The severity of the problem usually depends on the local climate and the diligence of the owner in detecting and ridding them from the dog and his housing. Because of their double coats, Siberian Huskies may harbor fleas and skin irritations that are not seen easily, so owners must routinely inspect the dog's skin, especially if the dog is scratching or biting

himself. Left unchecked, an afflicted dog can tear out layer and layer of coat and ultimately bloody his skin trying to relieve the itching.

The best way to control fleas is to prevent them by giving the dog a monthly dose of Lufenuron or Nitenpyram, which is marketed under several product names. Once in the bloodstream, the medicine is ingested by the flea whenever it bites the dog. The medicine interrupts the flea's reproduction cycle by preventing it from producing viable eggs. However, the medicine will not kill adult fleas, so it will take several weeks to take effect on an already infected animal. Because it causes stomach upset in some animals the pill should be given with a meal.

Another preventive measure is to put a topical flea treatment or a liquid insecticide into the dog's coat before infestation. This chemical is applied along the dog's back and tail and then combed through the coat. It must be reapplied at regular intervals. Although this procedure is not inexpensive, it has been highly effective for many dogs.

Despite your best efforts, if your dog does get a minor infestation, you can attempt to remove the fleas "naturally" by thoroughly brushing the dog's coat using a flea comb. This comb has thin blades that expose the fleas when you glide the comb along the skin. With the Siberian's thick coat and undercoat, this is all but impossible. Most owners use the powders and sprays designed specifically to kill fleas. They can be purchased at pet stores or grooming shops. The coat must be doused thoroughly with the repellent for it to work, and the active ingredient must reach the skin. Be extremely careful when applying the material. Cover the dog's eyes, nose, mouth, and ears, and slowly work the insecticide into the coat, working against the grain.

For heavy infestations, a flea dip bath will be needed. Many grooming parlors will do this, or you can do it at home. Always use products designed just for this purpose, and read all directions before beginning.

Once the dog has been ridded of fleas, you will have to ensure that the house, especially the dog's bedding, also is free of parasites and eggs. If the fleas are in the household carpeting, a heavy-duty insect bomb (available at most hardware stores and pet shops) will destroy all the breeding colonies.

A flea collar can provide a measure of protection from reinfection, but its powers are limited. Be sure to remove the collar if it gets wet, because it can become irritating to the skin.

Ticks

Ticks are another common problem that should not be taken lightly. They are disease carriers and can be painful for the afflicted dog. Once on their host, they gnaw through the skin and implant themselves so that they can suck and live off the dog's blood. One variety of tick, the deer tick, can induce Lyme disease in dogs as well as other animals and humans. If left untreated, this disease leads to arthritis, severe headaches, and heart problems.

Ticks are not detected easily on Siberian Huskies, because they are merely a fraction of an inch when they enter the dog's coat. Although flea and tick collars may help repel the parasite, they are only effective around the neck area. Infestations commonly occur on the hindquarters, around the tail, and around the ears.

A tick must be removed carefully. If simply ripped from the skin, the tick's head can tear away from the body and remain embedded in the skin, resulting in an infection or abscess. The proper way to remove a tick is to grasp it firmly using tweezers placed as close to the skin as possible. Wear protective gloves to minimize human exposure to such conditions as Lyme disease. Apply firm but gentle upward pressure. *Do not twist.* An alternative is to apply a tick dip, which can be purchased from most veterinarians or pet shops. This will, in effect, suffocate the tick and make it release its hold on the dog's skin. *Never try to burn a tick off with a match or a cigarette.* The dangers of this should be evident. Once a tick has been removed, a small lump or swollen area may remain for several days.

Lice and Mites

Several other types of external parasites can attack a dog, especially during the warm summer months. Lice or mite infestations are common and can result in uncontrollable itching and scratching in afflicted dogs. Because this can cause extensive damage to the dog's coat and skin that may take a long time to heal, it is important to catch skin problems in the early stages. If you notice any clusters of eggs, a rash of bumps, or pustules on the skin, consult your veterinarian for a proper diagnosis and treatment.

Stinging Insects

Bee and insect bites are difficult to detect. Many dogs will snap at a passing bee, oftentimes suffering the consequences. If you happen to witness your dog being bitten, or if you notice a sudden onset of limping, check the site and see if a stinger is still embedded. If it is, carefully remove it by scraping your fingernail or the side of a credit card across the base of the bite using a scooping motion. This will remove the stinger and limit the spread of the venom. Avoid squeezing the stinger, as it will release more toxins in the process. If possible, apply ice or a cold compress to reduce swelling. When possible, try to identify whether a wasp or a bee has stung your Siberian, because these insects produce different types of venom. A wasp has an alkaline-based venom, whereas a bee has an acidic venom. To neutralize the venom in a wasp sting, soak a pad or compress in vinegar and place it on the wound. For bee stings, make a paste of baking soda and water and place it atop the irritation.

Whereas an insect bite usually will be little more than a momentary discomfort for the dog, occasionally a dog will have an allergic reaction to a bite. Reactions will vary from dog to dog, depending on level of sensitivity. A case of hives or localized swelling gener-

ally will subside in a matter of hours, with no lasting effect. A more severe reaction, such as marked swelling or difficulty in breathing, requires immediate veterinary attention. For most cases, administering an over-the-counter antihistamine (as advised by your veterinarian) or a corticosteroid will relieve most symptoms. If your dog is allergic to stinging insects, consult with your veterinarian and devise a strategy for coping with future emergencies and have an antidote readily available at all times.

Common Health Problems

Siberian Huskies are adaptable to all types of weather and terrain. During their lives, most dogs will contract a few minor illnesses, and most of these should be no more serious than the passing upsets most humans must endure.

However, because dogs cannot communicate their discomforts, it is the owner's responsibility to monitor the dog's condition and make a decision about whether veterinary attention is required.

Diarrhea

A mild case of diarrhea may have many causes—most of which are not serious or life-threatening. The first step in treating this condition is to remove food from the dog for the next 12 to 24 hours to allow the dog's digestive system to rid itself of any offending material. A small amount of water or a tablespoon of Kaopectate is permissible. If symptoms do not worsen during the next 24 hours, the dog can be given several small, bland meals containing a binding agent, such as rice or oatmeal.

If you notice a bloody discharge or if the diarrhea continues for more than 48 hours, veterinary assistance is needed. Diarrhea combined with vomiting and/or a high fever can be symptomatic of a serious problem, so do not delay in getting help if the dog's condition seems to worsen.

Vomiting

Vomiting is caused by various illnesses that involve the digestive tract. Most incidents are quick to pass and often are related to something the dog has eaten or to viruses. Severe, continued vomiting is very serious, however, and can lead to dehydration.

If the vomiting is limited to only a few episodes, withhold all food for 12 to 24 hours, but let the dog have a little water or some ice chips. If there is no sign of fever and the vomiting subsides, you can give the dog several small servings of easily digestible foods, such as kibble with chicken broth, a little scrambled eggs, or rice, over the next 24 hours. If the vomiting does not recur, the normal diet can be resumed the following day. If vomiting continues or intensifies, or if you should notice any blood or worms in the vomit, consult a veterinarian immediately.

Some Siberian Huskies tend to gulp down their food. Because of a quick intake of air into the stomach, the dog may suddenly regurgitate the meal. For dogs prone to this behavior, the best solution is to serve several small meals each day rather than one or two large ones, thereby limiting the amount of food in the stomach at any one time.

Constipation

Constipation is more common in older dogs or in those that chew meat bones. It usually occurs after a dog undergoes a sudden change of diet. Confining a dog for too long a time may also cause this problem as the dog restrains his natural urges to eliminate until allowed outside. In such cases, the problem usually is temporary and can be alleviated by administering a mild laxative, such as Milk of Magnesia (ask your veterinarian for the proper dosage, based on your dog's weight).

If your dog is prone to constipation, add a little extra roughage or one tablespoon of mineral oil twice daily to his normal diet to aid proper elimination. If the condition lingers, your veterinarian may suggest using a glycerine suppository or a warm water enema to alleviate the blockage.

If you ever see the dog actively straining, crying out with pain, and not passing any excrement, seek professional care at once. The dog may have swallowed an object that is now lodged in the intestinal tract, causing a life-threatening situation. Alternatively, a tumor or other growth may be present in the intestines. These situations require specialized veterinary care.

Impacted Anal Glands

At the base of the dog's anus are two sacs that secrete a strong-smelling substance used by the dog as a scent marker. The anal sacs normally are emptied during defecation. If, however, they are not cleared completely by the normal elimination process, they can become impacted and will require manual emptying. This should be handled by your veterinarian, who will express the fluid and check it for pus or blood, which may indicate an infection.

The symptoms of impacted anal sacs include a constant licking of the area and/or dragging the anus across the ground or floor (this if often referred to as "scooting"). Check the dog carefully, as a dog may also scoot simply because there is feces collected in the anal hair.

If the anal sacs appear full, they can be expressed manually by carefully pressing along the outsides and back of the sacs with your thumb and forefinger positioned on either side of the gland. Be sure to hold a tissue below the gland to collect the fluid that flows out. If this procedure seems painful to the dog or if there is any pus or blood mixed in with the fluid, an infection may be present that will require veterinary attention.

Breed Anomalies

No dog breed of is totally free from genetic defects, but few breeds have as good a health record as the Siberian Husky. Not only are individual dogs generally healthy and good-tempered, but there has also been a relative lack of genetic issues throughout the years. The national breed club, the Siberian Husky Club of America, Inc. (SHCA), maintains a watchful eye for potential genetic problems and takes positive action when the general health and well-being of the breed has been challenged.

Since 1965, the SHCA has maintained a committee that researches the prevalence of genetic problems in the breed and alerts breeders before the defects begin to spread. Two major conditions have been uncovered in this manner: canine hip dysplasia and inheritable eye disease.

Hip Dysplasia

Hip dysplasia (HD) is a congenital malformation of the hip joint that causes an improper fit of the pelvic joint socket and the femur bone. While not present at birth, the condition develops during the first two years and is often progressive, causing inflammation, pain, and arthritis of the affected hip. It is aggravated by strenuous exercise, sitting up, lying down, or climbing stairs. Improper nutrition or overfeeding during the first year or two of life can increase the incidence of HD. In active dogs, such as the Siberian Husky, constant friction in an afflicted hip slowly wears the joint down, ultimately leading to pain when walking or during sudden movement. Although steps can be taken to relieve the pain and slow the course of the disease, there is no cure. Severely dysplastic dogs can be helped by hip surgery or hip replacement, but this is a painful and expensive solution. The first clinical signs of the disease generally do not appear until the dog is two to three years old, unless the animal is severely afflicted. Canine hip dysplasia's mode of inheritance is "polygenic," meaning it is due to a combination of multiple genes. Because of the nature of the disorder, some normal dogs produce a percentage of dysplastic offspring. The division of defective genes is uneven, with one parent contributing more defective genes than the other. Environmental factors, like a high caloric diet during puppyhood, can exacerbate changes in dysplastic hips but cannot create the condition.

Because HD is hereditary, the best way to eliminate the problem is by breeding only those dogs that are not predisposed for the disease. Unfortunately, some Siberian Husky lines have a tendency toward HD. It is estimated that 2 to 10 percent of today's Siberians have HD. Out of the 114 breeds identified as "at risk" for hip dysplasia, the Siberian Husky ranks among the least affected, coming in at 111 out of 114. This ranking is based upon evaluations from 1974 through 1994 and can be attributed to the cooperation of breeders who followed strict breeding program guidelines.

To protect the breed from this disease, breeders should have all dogs intended for breeding X-rayed when growth has stopped (at approximately 24 months of age). The dog is sedated and the hind limbs are rotated and extended to allow the proper positioning of the hips and femurs. It is recommended that bitches in heat or pregnant not be X-rayed, since the hormones may interfere with joint laxity. The X-rays are then sent for evaluation by specialists from the Orthopedic Foundation for Animals (OFA) or by three board-certified veterinary radiologists at a university veterinary school. The OFA will issue a certificate,

rating the condition of the hips. The final hip rating is decided by a consensus of the radiologists. Only dogs over 24 months of age that receive "excellent," "good," or "fair" evaluations receive an OFA registry number. This number is reported to the AKC and the parent breed club. Abnormal hips are reported to the owner and the referring veterinarian. Only those dogs certified as clear of the problem should be used in any breeding program. The X-rays should be repeated yearly, if the dog is to continue in a breeding program.

Unfortunately, although no guarantee exists that a dog will not develop HD, the chances can be minimized. All potential puppy buyers should ask to see the OFA registry papers of both the sire and dam of the litter. The OFA maintains a hip registry open to the public, which is also available on the OFA Web site (see page 92). Dogs that appear free of the disease can still pass along the trait if they carry a recessive gene for the trait.

Eye Disorders

While there are many possible eye defects, three conditions are of predominant concern in Siberians: hereditary or juvenile cataracts, corneal dystrophy, and progressive retinal atrophy (PRA). Each disorder is present in a different portion of the eye and can occur in dogs with any eye color. Eye defects in the Siberian Husky should be considered serious and should not be overlooked. If left unchecked, the dog will suffer a loss of acuity and eventual blindness. Of the three major eye diseases of the Siberian, hereditary cataracts are the most common, followed by corneal dystrophy and PRA. A report conducted by the American College of Veterinary Ophthalmologists showed that out of 1,345 Siberians examined, 107 dogs had inheritable cataracts (8%), 44 dogs had corneal dystrophy (3%), and 4 dogs had progressive retinal atrophy (less than 1%). Ask your breeder if there have been any cases of this associated with his or her stock (a reputable breeder will tell you if this has happened and what was done to eliminate the problem from their breeding stock).

Remind your veterinarian to check your Siberian's eyes carefully at the annual exam. If there is any hint of a problem, the dog should be taken to a veterinary ophthalmologist. To make owners aware of this problem, many local breed clubs sponsor clinics to help diagnose these conditions.

Hereditary Cataracts Hereditary cataracts are characterized by an opacity in the lens of the eye; it can occur in Siberians as young as three months of age. This disorder differs from non-hereditary cataracts, which tends to affect senior dogs. The function of the eye's lens is to focus rays of light, allowing the formation of an image on the retina. A cataract on the lens causes less light to enter the eye and can cause anything from a mild decrease in eyesight to complete blindness. The most common hereditary cataract in the Siberian Husky occurs on the posterior region of the lens, and it is not uncommon for a cataract to develop in one eye months before the other eye shows any effect of the disease. Recent DNA research indicates that juvenile cataracts may be carried by a recessive gene, and genetic research is under way to develop a simple DNA test to identify dogs that carry this gene.

Corneal Dystrophy As the name suggests, corneal dystrophy affects the cornea, which is the outer, transparent portion of the eyeball.

In most cases, Siberians with this disorder have an abnormal collection of lipids in the cornea, resulting in a hazy or crystalline opacity. Ophthalmologists describe the location of the opacity as anterior, mid-, or deep stromal. The Siberian is prone to deep stromal dystrophy, which involves triglyceride deposits. Annular dystrophy can also be present in Siberians, and this appears as a doughnut-shaped opacity in the peripheral cornea. Corneal dystrophy is usually seen in young adult dogs and tends to affect females more than males. Vision is seldom affected, and no effective therapy for the condition exists at this time. Recent genetic tests are suggesting that a recessive gene with variant expression transmits this disorder.

Progressive Retinal Atrophy (PRA) PRA affects the retina, the light-sensitive inner lining of the eye. The retina contains two types of specialized cells: rods and cones. The rods are necessary for vision in dim light, and the cones are utilized in bright light vision. The Siberian has a unique type of PRA that is only found in this breed as well as in humans. This type of PRA is called XLPRA ("X-linked PRA"), as it is transmitted through the XX chromosome of the female. XLPRA causes a loss of night vision, followed by a loss of day vision and eventually blindness. For male Siberians, the disease can be devastating, with loss of vision as early as five months of age. (For more information on screening programs, see page 92.)

Emergency Procedures

In emergency situations, speed is most important. Look up your closest 24-hour emergency services veterinary hospital, and have that contact information readily available. If your dog sustains a serious injury, your first act must be to calm and restrain the dog so that he cannot move and cause further damage to himself before you can transport him to a veterinarian.

You must also protect yourself from being bitten. Because the dog is terrified and may instinctively lash out at anyone who comes near him, be sure to approach the animal cautiously. Speak to him in low, soothing tones. A stocking, a tie, or a thin piece of cloth will serve as an emergency muzzle. (You should never use a muzzle on a dog that has chest injuries or is having difficulty breathing, however.) Fold the material in half and place a knot at the midpoint. Make a second loop approximately 6 inches (15.2 cm) above the knot, and place the dog's muzzle in the hole formed between the two. Pull the top loop tight over the muzzle, with the knot remaining above the jaw. Take the two ends and cross them under the jaw and around to the back of the head. Tie a secure knot, but be sure it is not too restrictive. You are now ready to assess the dog's physical condition.

Inspect the skin and locate the source of any bleeding. If possible, gently wash the area with soap and warm water. If the blood flow continues, apply a clean cloth or gauze pad to the site, secure it if possible, and hold the compress in place until the bleeding subsides. Unless the cut is very small, it will need professional attention. A veterinarian will be better able to apply a bandage that will stay in place.

If it appears that a bone has been broken, immobilize the dog to the best of your ability. If allowed to move, the dog may do damage to the muscles, cartilage, and nerves surrounding the break. Try to keep the dog calm, and get him to emergency treatment as quickly as possible. If necessary, you can use a blanket as a makeshift stretcher for transporting the dog short distances.

If the dog lapses into unconsciousness, check that his breathing passages are open. Get the dog onto his side. Gently pry open his mouth, and pull the tongue forward to allow airflow into the lungs.

In all of these situations, shock can quickly set in. Cover the dog with a blanket for added warmth, and monitor his heart rate. Never give an injured dog anything to eat or drink.

Poisonings

Most accidental poisonings occur without the owner ever knowing that the dog has ingested a poisonous substance. This often has serious consequences, as *immediate* action is required if the dog is to survive a serious poisoning. Symptoms of poisoning include diarrhea, vomiting, lethargy, spasms, shaking, dizziness, and a color change or bleeding of the mucous membranes.

If you know the cause of the poisoning and have the packaging, you may be able to look for information regarding the proper antidote. Your local poison control center may also be of help. It will help your veterinarian greatly to know how much poison was ingested and when, so as to formulate the proper method for removing it from the dog's system. Various procedures are used, depending on what type of poison has been ingested. Sometimes the stomach is pumped; sometimes the poison is neutralized in the stomach.

Household items are the most common sources of poisoning. Keep all cleaning agents, pesticides, and painting supplies locked up. Antifreeze is particularly dangerous, as it is highly poisonous but has a pleasant odor and taste that attract the dog. Many house and garden plants are poisonous if chewed or eaten. Included among these are philodendron, poinsettia, and daffodil bulbs.

Caring for Elderly Siberians

With good basic care throughout his life, your Siberian should remain vigorous and healthy for many years. As he ages, his digestive system probably will be the first to give him problems. Although constipation is common (often because of prostate problems), changes in the dog's diet can help alleviate this. Dogs over eight years of age should receive a premium diet specifically formulated for the digestive systems of older dogs. These foods generally contain easily digested meats and a lower level of protein. Your veterinarian may also suggest that you add several teaspoons of bran to the dog's daily meal and may prescribe vitamin supplements, especially if the dog appears lethargic. An adequate supply of water should always be available.

Elderly dogs tend to lose weight slowly, which can be the first sign of a degeneration of the ability of the liver and kidneys to properly manage waste materials. If you notice a weight loss, be sure to have the dog checked by your veterinarian to rule out any life-threatening condition.

The elderly dog may have sensitive teeth, and this inevitably will cause him to stop the heavy chewing that removes tartar. Although a weekly brushing of the teeth can minimize this, plaque removal by your veterinarian often is required.

Arthritis is common for many dogs and can be aggravated in a dog that has been active throughout his life, or in one that has become overweight. If your dog is bothered by this condition, avoid letting him climb stairs whenever possible, consider a ramp to help him climb into the car, and do not play games that require sudden turns or jumps.

TRAINING YOUR SIBERIAN HUSKY

Once your Siberian has mastered the basics, you can proceed to advanced training, such as sledding.

Leadership Position

Regardless of breed or sex, dogs—as pack animals—exhibit a consistent pattern of behavior that affects the training process, and every Siberian Husky owner who wants a well-mannered dog must recognize this. Siberian Husky or Chihuahua, it's really all the same: A dog will assume that he is the boss until proven otherwise. I call this the "leader-of-the-pack syndrome."

At birth, the dam assumes the leadership position in her pack and keeps her young in line. As the puppies begin to assert their independence, she will remind them of their place through low growls, a swat of the paw, or an occasional shake of the neck. Little else is necessary. She admonishes her young swiftly, fairly, consistently, and unemotionally, and they respect her position as leader. The wise owner follows the dam's example.

Consistency and Respect

Basic obedience training should begin as soon as your Siberian is taken into your home (see "The Basic Commands," pages 81–87), with formal obedience training from an experienced instructor beginning at approximately six months of age and continuing with weekly group lessons until at least a year old, when your dog can perform unfailingly in all situations. Many Siberians exhibit a stubborn streak, making obedience training all the more important and proactive. If you are not willing to invest the time needed to fully train your dog in proper behavior, **the Siberian is not the breed for you.**

If the dog misbehaves, respond accordingly and appropriately. Consistency is vital. Letting a dog's "cute little antics" go uncorrected will undermine an owner's leadership position and encourage the dog to misbehave again.

Respond firmly but fairly every time the dog acts up, letting him know what behavior is expected and what will not be tolerated. Brute force is not required and is extremely counterproductive. The Siberian is a spirited breed and undoubtedly will test his owner's authority occasionally. When this happens, correct in a manner the dog will understand—a firm vocal reprimand, a stern look, a quick shake of the neck with your hand (being careful to just surprise the dog, not injure it). Correct him as his mother would, as the dog already should understand the method and the meaning. Little more should be necessary to make your displeasure clear if you are carrying out the corrections authoritatively. Be sure never to whine, nag, plead, or preach at the dog, as these clearly are not the actions of a leader, and the dog will not feel compelled to obey.

Although this may sound more like psychology than discipline or training, please keep in mind that obedience is based on respect. The dog must respect you, or he will not obey (unless out of fear, which is totally destructive to the owner/dog bond). The lessons that follow are general outlines regarding how to teach and discipline your dog in a way that will yield a well-mannered companion.

Rules to Train By

It is useless and frustrating to begin training a puppy before he is capable of understanding what you want. However, lessons in good house manners can begin when the dog first enters the home. The dog's first successes can be learning and responding to his name, coming when called, catching on to what *"No!"* means, and starting to learn the *sit.* Concen-

tration is the key. If the puppy constantly wanders off, either physically or mentally, he is probably too young for formal training.

The lessons should be short at first, about five to ten minutes, but held *regularly,* two or three times each day. Repeat all lessons frequently, but not to a point where the dog can no longer concentrate or show interest. Boredom can do serious damage to a training program, and Siberians can get bored easily.

The atmosphere should be serious, but not unpleasant. Encourage the dog to perform well for you. Praise each minor success, but don't go overboard and make the dog so excited that he forgets the purpose of your time together.

All commands should be given with a firm, authoritative tone of voice. The tone is very important. Be careful not to sound as if you continually are scolding the dog or, even worse, pleading. Be sure to issue the same command each time you request a certain action (not *"Jax, come"* one time and *"Come here, boy"* the next). The simpler the better. As a general rule, you should include the dog's name in any command requiring motion *(come, heel)* but omit it from the commands that require the dog to remain motionless *(sit, stay, down).* Hand cues can also be an effective training aid and should be used in conjunction with verbal commands. For example, to help your Siberian learn the *sit* command, make a pointing motion toward the ground when vocalizing the command. By positioning your hand above your Siberian's head, his attention will be drawn backwards; many Siberians will fall into the sit position instinctually. Other hands cues, such an extended palm (the "stop" hand motion), can be effective for the *stay* command. For creative training methods, you could also point your finger in a gun shape and use the verbal command "bang" to incite your dog to the down or "play dead" position.

To be effective, each mistake must be corrected immediately with a verbal, *"No!"* Repeat the command, show the dog the proper response, and praise him when successful. Try to keep your talking to a minimum. Use simple, clear commands, and repeat the command only when necessary. Your goal is to have the dog respond correctly after only one command. A dog that needs constant prompting is not responding correctly. Reward correct behavior with affection, edible treats, or giving a favorite toy.

Progress slowly, as an action quickly learned often is forgotten quickly. Build each day on the success of the previous lesson. Patience and consistency are the keys to success. Many repetitions are necessary before the dog can be expected to truly understand how he is to respond to any given command. Patience and consistency is key.

Regardless of how smart or willing the dog, mistakes will be made throughout the learning process. Correct fairly and with love, not out of anger. The dog most likely is making mistakes out of confusion, not willful misbehavior. Never shout at or strike the dog, as this will only worsen matters. Emphasize the dog's successes rather than his mistakes.

By keeping the lessons short and pleasant, the dog will remain eager to learn. Do not be tempted to push the dog beyond his capabilities, even if things are going well, as this can lead to exhaustion and disinterest.

End each lesson with a lot of verbal praise and petting, and turn to a pleasant activity, such as a walk, a run, or a game. Giving the dog a little special attention after a job well done lets the dog know you are pleased with his performance. With such positive reinforcement the dog will learn to regard training as pleasurable, not as a drudgery.

Training Puppies

Although Siberian Huskies can be quite adept at learning, they can also get bored and distracted easily. All training must enforce the idea that learning can be fun and will bring positive responses from the owner, but it must be clear from the start that training is not a game. It need not be unpleasant, however. Early successes—and a little creativity by the owner—are the keys to piquing and sustaining interest in training.

Although it may sound elementary, getting the dog to respond to his name is an important lesson. This task is accomplished easily by using the dog's name whenever you want him to come, and by praising the dog lavishly when he responds. The dog will react happily to the attention he is getting and will subconsciously note how you react when you are pleased. This is the puppy's first success. He discovers that a correct response brings rewards. Siberians Huskies thrive on such positive reinforcement. The dog bonds to you and learns to want to please you, despite his "opportunistic" and primal tendencies. The dog's desire to please his owner is the backbone of a training program and must always be fostered.

The Primary Tools

Collars

Although you may want to familiarize the young puppy with the feel of a collar by hav-

Choose a collar that is the correct size for the dog—not one he will grow into. The collar should measure approximately 1 to 2 inches (2.5–5 cm) more than the diameter of the dog's head. A choke collar is designed to provide quick, snap-tight corrections. It is pointless to buy oversized collars because they will not close quickly and can, in fact, be dangerous if allowed to hang down loosely.

To form the collar, slip the chain through one of the rings. The leash can then be attached to the free ring. The side of the chain connecting to the free ring must be placed over the top of the neck once it's on, not under. In this position, the collar instantly will release whenever the upward pressure is removed. Although few Siberians complain when given a collar, you might want to let the dog wear it for a day to get accustomed to the added weight around his neck.

Lightweight Collars. If you want your dog to wear identification, select a lightweight collar that can be left on the dog at all times. There are also safety collars available for both puppies and adult dogs. Safety collars have a clasp designed to come apart if the collar becomes stuck or put under pressure, and they are designed to minimize strangulation hazards. Attach a small metal medallion listing the dog and owner's names, address, phone number, and any health problems the dog may have. These can be purchased at pet stores. If your dog is registered with a microchip service, have that information tag displayed as well.

Training Leashes

The training leash is made generally of nylon, woven cloth, or leather. Most people use a 6-foot (1.8-m) lead, ½ to 1 inch (1.3–2.5

ing him wear a lightweight one when young, no collar really is necessary until formal training is to begin. However, if your puppy will ever be outside of your home or immediate care, he should be wearing identification tags. When the dog has matured enough for formal training, you may need a training or choke collar, which consists of metal links with a ring on each end. This collar should be worn only during teaching sessions. It allows you to apply as much pressure as necessary to evoke the correct response or action by the dog. When pulled upward, the collar will tighten momentarily around the dog's neck. Once the pressure is released, it will loosen immediately. The dog will learn quickly that the upward tug indicates displeasure and that a correction is needed. The choke collar is a valuable teaching aid that should never be used to hurt the dog.

cm) in width, although a 3-foot (1.2-m) leash sometimes is used when more control is necessary. If the dog tries to chew the leash, correct with a firm *"No!"* and give the leash a light upward tug to remove it from the dog's grasp. Many puppies will feel awkward and frightened by the tug of this sudden weight around their necks, so you may want to let the puppy drag the leash behind him for a short time. Monitor the situation closely in case the dog becomes frightened and to make sure he does not get tangled and possibly hurt.

Once your Siberian has adapted to the feel of the leash, pick up the leash but apply no overt pressure on the dog's collar. Walk around with the puppy for several minutes, following wherever he wanders. Now let the pup know it is time to follow you. If all is progressing well, introduce the feel of the upward tug whenever the puppy moves out and tries to pull on the leash. The puppy usually will be stunned by this intrusion—sometimes annoyed. Reassure him that there is nothing to be afraid of, but continue to apply firm pressure whenever he wanders out of your control area. Using quick corrections, you should be able to make it clear to the puppy that the leash is a restraint and that the tugs require corrective action on his part. Never tug abruptly or jolt the leash with excessive force, as it could cause bodily injury to your dog. Once this is clear, formal obedience lessons can begin.

The Basic Commands

Regardless of how you intend to use your Siberian Husky, he must learn five basic commands: *sit, stay, heel, come,* and *down.* Until a dog willingly performs these commands, he should be considered untrustworthy and should be removed from activities where self-control is required. This is not punishment; it is restraint. Participation should be the dog's reward for learning proper behavior and self-restraint. Siberians have a high predatory instinct and should be kept on a leash whenever it is in an unfamiliar or unenclosed environment.

Owners are responsible for teaching their Siberians the basic commands. Siberian Huskies are, by nature, quite intelligent and can be capable learners if the owner knows how to keep the dog's attention and interest. Your task is to teach your dog to obey you instantly, with only one command. Accept no less, as the Siberian will most likely try to get away with a less-than-perfect performance if you let him, as there is a definite stubborn streak in the breed.

Siberian Huskies are not known for their concentration powers, so make the task as easy as possible for everyone involved by practicing the early lessons indoors, in an area free from distractions. The dog should be on a leash for all of the basic exercises.

Sit

When performing properly, the dog will sit at your left side, with his shoulders square to your knee. Position the dog at your side, with the leash in your right hand. Keep the leash taut, applying a slight amount of upward pressure to help keep the dog's head up. Command the dog *"Sit"* while you press your left hand on his rear and place him in the sitting position. If the dog moves out of position, use your left

hand to straighten him while your right hand continues the moderate upward pressure from the leash. Praise the dog when he is properly positioned, and release with *"Good dog!"* and/or an upward sweep of your left hand.

It is important to praise the dog when he reaches the *sit* position, not when he gets up. He must learn to associate the praise with the sitting action.

The first *sits* should be quite short, so that the dog has little chance to tire of the position and slump over on your leg or lie down. You want to emphasize success. Gradually increase the *sit* time. If the dog moves out of position, correct with *"No!"* and a light jerk from the leash, then put him back in place.

Once the sitting action becomes habitual in response to the command, there should be no need for you to touch or press on the dog's rear. At this point you can begin training the *stay* and *heel* commands.

Stay

You should not begin teaching the *stay* command until the dog reliably is performing the *sit*. The *stay* command builds from the *sit*. Place the dog in a *sit*, keeping some upward pressure on his neck from the leash in your right hand. As you command *"Stay!"* you simultaneously take one step away from the dog, beginning your movement with your right leg (which is the furthest from the dog). Bring the palm of your left hand down toward his face, stopping just short of his muzzle. The hand signal must be made at the same time that the command is given and the step is taken. Retain eye contact, if possible. Repeat the command while maintaining the signal in a voice that is firm and authoritative.

Do not expect the dog to stay for more than ten seconds or so at first, so release after a small success and praise.

When the dog breaks the *stay*, return him immediately to the *sit* and repeat the whole procedure. Your Siberian will undoubtedly try to move toward you once he sees you move away, or he will try to lie down. Be patient and do not expect immediate results. Correct each infraction and try again, but do not bore the dog with endless repetitions. Move on to another exercise, and spring the *stay* on the dog every now and then—not continuously. Praise each minor success lavishly.

Slowly extend the length of the *stay* and the distance you move away from the dog each time. A well-trained dog can be relied on to stay in the *sit* position for several minutes.

Placing the dog in a *sit-stay* is an excellent way to deal with the breed's natural desire to jump up and greet visitors. Whenever a visitor comes to the door, make the dog sit through-out the initial greeting. If possible, have one person stay with the dog while another answers the door. Have the newcomer ignore the dog at first, as this will lower the dog's interest in jumping. As the dog matures and masters the proper greeting, you will hopefully not have to resort to an extended *stay* when-ever someone comes to your door.

Heel

An untrained Siberian Husky will surely surge ahead of his owner when on a leash, pulling the hapless owner along for a ride. This bad habit should not be tolerated and must be stopped while the dog is still young. Heeling is no more than a controlled walk, and every Siberian should be required to perform it.

Always place the dog on your left side, his chest preferably in line with knee. Hold the leash in your right hand and use your left to supply corrective jerks.

The *heel* starts with the dog in a *sit*. Move out with your left foot first, commanding *"Jax, Heel!"* as you move forward. Snap the leash as you give the command to start him forward, removing the pressure as he responds. Walk at a comfortable pace, and jerk the lead only if he surges ahead or lags behind. Make your snaps quick and firm, and repeat *"Heel!"* with each correction. Praise the dog as soon as he responds, using a pleasant tone and *"Good boy!"* Repeat the praise as you are

═CHECKLIST═

Problem Solving

When training problems are encountered, ask yourself these questions:

✔ Are your commands clear, concise, and consistent?

✔ Are you giving the dog ample time to learn, not rushing him?

✔ Do you speak in a firm, authoritative tone (never shouting, scolding, or whining)?

✔ Do you praise the dog enough to make learning a pleasant experience?

✔ Are **you** concentrating?

If you feel the problem is with the student and not the teacher, observe the dog's behavior and body language.

✔ **Is the dog easily distracted?** This is very typical of Siberian Huskies. You may be training in an area that presents too many distractions. Try a more secluded training site and see if the dog's concentration improves.

✔ **Is this lapse a new or constant occurrence?** A sudden disinterest or confusion in a male can be caused by a local bitch in heat. Alternatively, the dog may have reached a temporary learning plateau (common during the fifth or sixth week of training) and may appear to have forgotten all he has learned. This odd phenomenon is not unusual and generally passes in a week.

✔ **Is the dog ill?** Many illnesses are hard to spot. A dog that is reluctant to move freely or jump may be showing the early signs of HD (see page 71). Eliminate the health issue with a thorough examination by a veterinarian.

moving if the dog remains in proper position, but don't overdo it and interfere with the dog's concentration.

When you stop, the dog is to sit at your side. In the beginning you will need to issue the *sit* command; however, as the dog becomes adept at heeling the *sit* should become automatic when you stop and no verbal command should be needed.

Learning the *heel* will take time, and your Siberian may lose his concentration quite frequently. As you encounter problems—usually surging ahead—you may have to stop and place the dog in a *sit* to restore calm. This certainly is preferable to continually snapping the dog back into position, and it allows the dog to succeed at a task he already is familiar with, and thereby receive praise. This will keep everyone at ease and help the heeling practice continue rather than break down into confusion on the dog's part and anger on the owner's. Once the dog successfully has completed the *sit*, move out again with *"Jax, heel!"* Praise if he comes and moves in the proper position. Stop as soon as he misbehaves, giving a firm tug on the leash and a stern *"no."*

If the dog continues to surge, you must continue to break this pattern by stopping. Do not apply continuous pressure from the leash on the neck of a surging dog, as this will mean that the choke continually is applied. The choke should be used sparingly to regain the dog's attention and bring about a correction. It is to be used only when needed and should be released immediately. Many Siberians are impervious to the shock of the snap of the standard choke chain. I've had good results by adding a startling sound in addition to the corrective neck jerk, which is accomplished by just slapping my own thigh to make a popping sound. If this doesn't work with your dog, you may need to consult a professional trainer in your area about selecting a more effective training collar for your dog.

Keep the early heeling attempts short—no more than 10 to 15 minutes. When the dog becomes more adept and no longer needs to be put into frequent corrective *sits,* you can extend the lessons as energy and interest permit. Once you get the dog to heel properly and not surge, the walk will become a great time to share each other's company.

Come

The *come* is relatively easy to teach, as Siberian Huskies instinctively will respond to the sound of their master's voice and will seek out the sound. The *come* teaches a dog that he must return to his master at once, without hesitation.

In most situations, even puppies happily come when called, in anticipation of play, food, or various pleasant exchanges. The biggest obstacle to overcome is what I call the "What's in it for me?" syndrome. The goal of the *come* command is to structure this response so that the dog will obey your call regardless of the circumstances.

Begin training the *come* command with a pleasant play period. Place the dog on a long leash or rope (20 feet [6.1 m] or more works best) and let him play in the practice yard. Hold the leash but maintain only minimal tension. Once the dog is relaxed and occupied with some nearby object, command *"Jax, come!"* in a firm tone, and snap the leash to start the dog moving toward you. Praise as the dog *begins* to move. Have him come directly to you and into a *sit.* Should he fail to respond, give a

sharp correction with the leash and repeat *"Jax, come!"* If necessary, repeat the command and reel the dog in by slowly retracting the cord (but this rarely is required).

Once the dog has completed the *come* and gotten into a proper *sit,* release with *"Good boy!"* and let him roam once more. Repeat the command at various intervals, and enforce with a sharp tug on the leash should the dog ever fail to move toward you immediately.

The *come* should be used and practiced only sparingly. Although you should test the dog on it no more than once or twice in a training session, you can use it at various points throughout the day when the dog's presence really is requested. Praise highly when the dog responds and do not allow the dog to ever ignore the command.

If you need to correct your dog for an offense of any kind, *go to him* and reprimand. *Never command the dog to come and then punish him when he arrives.* If you call the dog with *"Come!"* and then proceed to punish him when he arrives, you almost certainly will ruin your chances of having a dog that instantly will return to you when called, thus negating this command's importance and reliability.

Down

The *down* command builds from the *sit* and *stay* commands. To teach your Siberian Husky to lie down, begin by placing him in a *sit* while you kneel by his side. As you command *"Down!"* grab his front legs near the body, gently lift them from the floor, and lower the dog to the ground. Once down, command the dog to *"Down, stay!"* Praise with *"Good boy"* if he remains in the prone position. Your left hand can rest on the dog's back to deter him from getting up, if necessary. Release from the *down* by motioning upward with your hand and gently tugging the leash. The dog should then return to the *sit* position.

With this command, the downward movement needs to be reinforced, and the concept must clearly be differentiated from the *stay*. Do not make your dog remain in the *down* position too long at first, but be sure he remains lying on all fours. The dog is to be alert on the *down*, not overly sprawled out.

The *down* can be practiced several times each day. As the downward movement becomes more familiar, you no longer will need to lower the dog's legs. During this transition, try issuing the command and just slapping the floor with the palm of your hand to get the dog moving down. You also can try placing the leash under your left foot, keeping it rather taut, and as you command *"Down!"* add a slight pressure on the dog's shoulders to get him moving down.

As the dog progresses, teach him to lie down on the leash from various positions, such as in front of you or from a distance. It is very useful to incorporate a down motion with your hand at the time of the *down* command to augment these exercises. When working indoors, practice the *down* off leash. Never accept a sloppy performance once the leash is removed. This may sound a bit harsh, but a Siberian should never be allowed off leash in an unconfined outdoor area. An exciting scent or the sight of something moving in the distance may lure away even a well-trained and disciplined Siberian—and he can be nearly out of sight in just a moment's time.

It is good discipline to train the dog to perform an extended *down-stay* daily. With practice (and some Siberians need *lots* of practice at this), you will be able to have your dog remain in a *down-stay* for 30 minutes or more. This will reinforce your position as leader in the dog's mind and will give you the control you need at times to remove the dog from any undesirable activities (such as hanging around the dinner table or getting underfoot when company comes)—and you won't have to lock him up. A properly trained dog can be placed in an extended *down-stay* near his owner, yet in a place where he can relax too, such as across the room or in a corner.

Begin with *stays* of a few minutes and gradually increase the time, but do it irregularly (10 minutes, then 8 minutes the next time, 15 the next). With this approach, the dog cannot anticipate when he will be finished, and he truly will learn to obey the command.

Siberian Huskies invariably will become bored and try to break the *stay*. Tell him *"No, stay!"* and replace him. As the dog becomes accustomed to the long *down*, he often will fall asleep. This is perfectly acceptable as long as he remains where he was placed when he awakens. You should make it a point to wake the dog with a tap of the foot near his head when it is time for the release. Do not let him sleep on indefinitely, as you need to formally complete the exercise for it to have any impact. Always end the long *down-stay* with the upward release motion and then give the dog great praise, as this exercise requires a lot of self-control, which is not a cornerstone of the Siberian Husky temperament.

The "emergency" *down* also can be an effective lifesaving command to immediately stop a dog from participating in or entering into a dangerous situation. Once you are certain that the dog understands the *down* concept, the *down* can be practiced while walking, not just from the *sit*. Teaching a dog to drop on command while in motion takes time, but is well worth the effort. If your Siberian Husky somehow finds a way out of your yard and wanders near traffic, you could use the *down* to drop the dog immediately to the ground until you could retrieve him. Few Siberians have any car sense, and this command could save a dog's life. Such a case illustrates why only an *immediate* response to the command can be acceptable.

Training Problems

There are as many training methods as there are trainers, so rest assured that there is no foolproof method for training all dogs. Do not get discouraged if your dog is not learning as quickly and efficiently as you had expected. Various problems often arise that interfere with the learning process. Your dog may just not be able to adapt to the training method you have selected. Finding the solution to a training problem generally is a matter of trial and error and, most of all, patience and perseverance. The most obvious place to start is to evaluate your teaching technique.

If, despite your best efforts, disorder still prevails in your training program, consult a professional trainer (preferably one experienced with Siberian Huskies). An expert eye often can spot quickly if there is an underlying problem and propose corrective measures. Many times all that is needed is a new approach or technique that the dog will understand or like better. Sometimes the owner needs a lesson in how to better discipline the dog or keep his interest.

TIP

Giving Commands

• The trainer's tone of voice is very important. Each command should be firm and authoritative; you do not want to sound as if you are continually scolding the dog or—even worse—pleading with him.

• Many trainers include the dog's name in all commands that require motion (*"Jax, come!"* or *"Jax, heel!"*) but omit it for corrections and commands that require the dog to remain motionless (*"Sit," "Stay,"* or *"Down"*).

• Use the *same command* every time you request a certain action (not *"Jax, come!"* one time and *"Come here, boy!"* the next). Use whatever works best for you, as some dogs may react to *"Enough!"* or *"Thank you!"* better than *"No"* or *"Good boy!"* Once you've figured what works best for you and your dog, stick with it. Consistency and clarity are the most important factors.

• The word *"No"* is used so frequently that some dogs become immune to hearing it, so many trainers use *"Wrong!"* in reaction to a failure to comply to a command and a two-word reprimand—*"No jump!"* or *"No chew!"*—when the dog is about to misbehave or is caught in the act. Immediately correct each improper response, repeat the command, show the dog the proper response, and lavish with praise when successful.

• During lessons, try to keep your talking to a minimum. Use simple, clear commands and repeat them only when necessary.

Never let training setbacks—and there will be some—escalate to the point where you lash out at the dog or give up in despair. Help from a more experienced trainer usually is a good investment in your dog's future.

Advanced Training

Owners of Siberian Huskies will find that the breed can excel in many sports and types of competition.

Show-quality Siberian Huskies are among the most popular entries at AKC conformation shows (such as all-breed shows—like Westminster—or specialty shows, where only Siberians are judged). In this type of competition, the entrants are judged on their physical appearance against the guidelines of the breed standard. (See page 27.)

For training enthusiasts, Siberians can learn the skills required for Obedience competition. Obedience trials are held under AKC auspices, with competition at novice, open, and utility levels. There are training clubs dedicated strictly to this sport, and Obedience trials routinely are held in conjunction with most large AKC conformation shows. There are also some less common sports that are tailor-made for Siberian Huskies.

Sledding/Mushing

A sport in keeping with this breed's heritage is the sled dog degree program, which is administered by the SHCA. The goal is to demonstrate the ability of the Siberian Husky in sled dog racing competition. The program is open to all purebred Siberian Huskies individually registered with the AKC. Competition is in three degree levels, based on experience and distance. There are three types of races: sprint, distance, and triathlon.

The applicant canine must be a purebred, although the applicant may work as part of a mixed breed team. Spayed or neutered dogs are eligible, and all races must be on snow, with sleds held under the direction of a Recognized Race Giving Organization (RRGO), under all race rules, and with recorded results. Each individual application for a degree must include a copy of the dog's AKC registration papers; a completed Sled Dog Degree Program application from the SHCA; certified race results signed by Race Marshal, Chief Judge, or Timer; and printed race results that include date, finishing times, and placing.

The applicant dog must run the entire race as a member of the team, and no more than three races per season may be on the same trail. Applicants are encouraged to race in a variety of locations and against a diverse spectrum of competition.

There are three degree levels: Sled Dog (SD), which denotes a basic level of proficiency in sled racing and an accumulation of no less than 100 miles in five or more successfully completed races; Sled Dog Excellent (SDX), which recognizes a high level of proficiency in sled dog racing; and Sled Dog Outstanding (SDO), the highest honor for sledding dogs. Once a degree is completed and approved by the SHCA, the appropriate initials can be used after the dog's name. For more information on the Sled Dog Degree Program, contact the SHCA (see page 92).

Working Pack Dog Programs

The newest performance program sponsored by the SHCA is the Working Pack Dog Program, which recognizes the achievements of Siberian Huskies participating in verifiable hiking trips as an active member of the hiking party, such as cross country excursions, hiking trails, or back country hikes. Dogs in this program may compete for two titles: Working Pack Dog (WPD) and Working Pack Dog Excellent (WPDX). The dog must carry a canine pack with an initial weight equal to 25 percent of the dog's body weight. The pack may be lightened during the course of travel because of the consumption of food, water, and other supplies, but the ending load cannot be less than 10 percent of the body weight.

Another sport that utilizes the Siberian's innate ability to pull is skijoring, where one or two dogs pull a person on skies. The name is derived from the Norwegian word "*skikjøring*," which translates to "ski driving." The skier provides power via skis and poles, and the dog supplies additional momentum by running and pulling. The skier wears a skijoring harness, the dog wears a sled dog harness, and the two are connected by rope. There are no reins or signaling devices for control, so the dog must be motivated by his own desire to run and must respond to the skier's voice for direction.

Agility

Agility is a fast-paced sport in which the dog must navigate over various types of jumps, tunnels, and other obstacles. The dog and handler are working against the clock and other exhibitors. Agility originated in England and was brought to this country by the United States Dog Agility Association (USDAA). The AKC began sponsoring Agility trials in 1994. Many owners of Siberian Huskies find Agility a wonderful pastime with their pet.

Therapy Work

One of the most fulfilling activities a Siberian and his owner can engage in is therapy work. Research has proved that animals enrich the lives of humans in ways that can reduce stress and make them happier and healthier. Organizations throughout the world, such as Therapy Dogs International or the Delta Society, currently are engaged in developing programs in which well-trained dogs visit elderly, sick, or emotionally disturbed people, as well as prisoners. The dogs are therapeutic aids that can help people in many ways—as aids for those struggling to recover from debilitating illnesses, such as a stroke, or as loving enticements for withdrawn and uncommunicative children. This pet-facilitated therapy has proved highly successful.

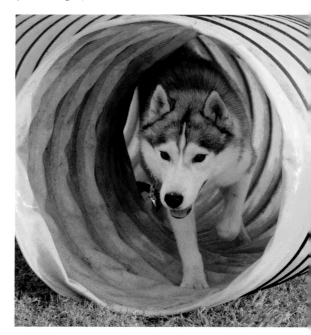

HOW-TO: HOUSETRAINING

The first thing to know about housetraining is *when* the puppy will need to eliminate: after waking, after eating, after strenuous play, first thing in the morning, and last thing at night. There also will be in-between times, and the puppy usually will give some physical cues: he looks uneasy, sniffs the ground, and walks in circles, as if searching for something. Take your puppy outside to the designated area every hour, if possible. This practice and repetition seems to help train the dog to eliminate on command, whether he feels the desire or not. During the early housetraining stages, your puppy should be in his crate when not being monitored by a responsible party. Quick housetraining depends in large part on the attentiveness of the owner: knowing when the puppy will need to eliminate, monitoring his physical signs, getting him to the proper elimination area in time, and praising every success.

Until four to six months of age, a puppy has limited bladder control. And until a puppy truly understands what is expected, mistakes are inevitable. The owner must react in a firm and fair manner the

puppy will understand. Do not overreact when you find an unwanted deposit. To make a connection in the dog's mind with your displeasure and the waste, bring the dog to the spot. Point at the excrement and have him look. Scold in a low, guttural tone. Immediately bring the dog to the proper elimination area. Praise the dog if he eliminates. When you both return to the house, clean up the mess out of the dog's sight. *Never hit the dog or rub his nose in excrement.*

To avoid having a stain that reattracts the dog to the spot, be sure to wash each accident site with a cleaning solution designed to specifically remove urine odors. Do not use an ammonia-based cleaner, as this may reattract the dog to the spot.

Aiding the Task

During the training period, make the extra effort and go out with the puppy. He needs instruction on where to go and, most of all, praise when he succeeds.

Restrict where the puppy may go until he is reliably housetrained. When not under direct supervision, the dog should be confined to two

areas: the sleeping quarters and the elimination area. The sleeping quarters should be a small, uncarpeted, puppy-proof area with all escape routes blocked off. A mesh baby gate will do well while the puppy is small. The elimination area should be outside, rather than a papered area in the house. Paper training, or lining the floor with "training pads," should be avoided if at all possible; outdoor training should be encouraged from the puppy's first days in the home. Bring the puppy to the elimination area each time he shows signs of needing to go. Stay with the puppy and encourage him with *"Do your business"* or any similar phrase that does not include the terms *come, sit,* or *down,* which will be used later as obedience commands. Praise the puppy enthusiastically whenever he goes. Your dog should learn quickly that this spot is acceptable for elimination—and that you are pleased when he goes there.

Picking Up Waste

In most cities, owners who do not clean up after their pets are subject to fines ranging from $50 to $500. Cleaning up dog waste not only rids the streets, lawns, and public areas of repugnant and potentially harmful materials, but it also proves that dog owners have good manners.

"Pooper-scoopers" designed for picking up waste are available in pet stores, or the job can be accomplished easily—and sanitarily—using an inverted plastic bag, which you knot and then throw in a covered container.

Crates

A crate is the most efficient method of housetraining. As pack animals, dogs instinctively seek out the confinement and security of a den.

Well-constructed dog crates are made of heavy-duty plastic or wire mesh and can be purchased from pet stores. The crate must be large enough for the dog to comfortably sit or lie down in, but not so large as to give the dog plenty of room to subdivide his confines into a bed area and an elimination area.

A crate can be a valuable housetraining tool when used in conjunction with a regular schedule of walks and feedings. The owner must take the dog to his proper elimination area at regular intervals and enthusiastically praise the dog each time he relieves himself there.

Although the owner may remain in the room with the puppy during the first few cratings to help him feel at ease, occupy yourself with an activity and pay no outward attention to the puppy unless there are signs of distress. Siberian Huskies are very intuitive, and if they sense anxiety or guilt in their owner's behavior, they may use this to their advantage. Alternatively, they may decide that the crate really is something to be afraid of because their owner is obviously upset by it.

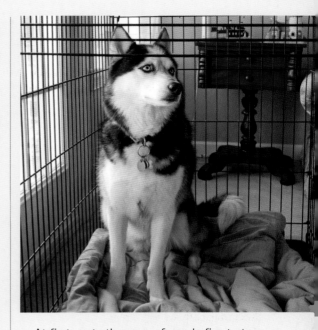

At first, crate the puppy for only five to ten minutes. This time can be increased gradually over the next few weeks. During the day, puppies under 12 weeks of age may remain in the crate for up to one hour; puppies 12 to 16 weeks of age may be crated for up to two hours; older puppies may stay a maximum of three to four hours in a crate. The time a dog spends in his crate should be based on the dog's age and elimination requirements and will vary from dog to dog. All ages can be crated overnight.

The crate should be situated out of household traffic but not somewhere that will make the dog feel isolated. Line the bottom of the crate with a blanket for added comfort and give the dog a chew toy or bone to help relieve boredom. Bowls of food or water do not belong in the crate during the housetraining process.

INFORMATION

Organizations

American Society for the Prevention of
Cruelty to Animals (ASPCA)
424 East 92nd Street
New York, NY 10128
www.aspca.org

American Veterinary Medical Association
1931 N. Meacham Road
Schaumberg, IL 60173
www.avma.org

Canine Eye Registration Foundation (CERF)
1248 Lynn Hall
Purdue University
West Lafayette, IN 47907
www.vmdb.org/cerf.html

The Delta Society
875 124th Avenue NE
Bellevue, WA 98005
www.deltasociety.org

Humane Society of the United States
2100 L Street N.W.
Washington, DC 20037
www.humanesociety.org

International Siberian Husky Club
E-mail (rhpbthomas@gmail.com)
www.ishclub.org

Orthopedic Foundation for Animals (OFA)
2300 East Nifong Boulevard
Columbia, MO 65201
www.offa.org

Pet Care Services Association
2760 N. Academy Boulevard, Suite 120
Colorado Springs, CO 80917
www.petcareservices.org

Siberian Husky Club of America, Inc.
Barbara Horsey, Corresponding Secretary
10194 Old Kent Lane
Clarkston, MI 48348
E-mail: bhorseyshca@gmail.com
www.shca.org
(Since new officers are elected periodically,
contact the group for the latest information.)

Siberian Husky Club of Canada
E-mail: *info@siberianhuskyclubofcanada.com*
www.siberianhuskyclubofcanada.com/

Siberian Husky Ophthalmic Registry (SHOR)
Jamesa Maulden, SHOR Chairperson
PO Box 1109
Maple Valley, WA 98038-1109
E-mail: jamesa@syntari.com
www.shca.org/shcahp7.htm
(Since new officers are elected periodically,
contact the group for the latest information.)

The Seeing Eye
10 Washington Valley Road
Morristown, NJ 07960
www.seeingeye.org

Therapy Dogs International
88 Bartley Road
Flanders, NJ 07836
www.tdi-dog.org

International Kennel Clubs

The American Kennel Club (AKC)
260 Madison Avenue
New York, NY 10016
www.akc.org

United Kennel Club
100 East Kilgore Road
Kalamazoo, MI 49001
www.ukcdogs.com

The Kennel Club
1-4 Clargis Street Picadilly
London W7Y 8AB England
www.the-kennel-club.org.uk

Canadian Kennel Club
200 Ronson Drive, Suite 400
Etokicoke, Ontario M9W 5Z9 Canada
www.ckc.ca

Australian National Kennel Council
www.ankc.org

Irish Kennel Club
Fottrell House, Harolds X Bridge
Dublin 6W Ireland
http://ikc.ie

New Zealand Kennel Club
Prosser St., Private Bag 50903
Porirva, 5240 New Zealand
www.nzkc.org.nz

Books

American Kennel Club. *The Complete Dog Book.* New York: Macmillan, 1992.

Baer, Ted. *Communicating with Your Dog.* Hauppauge, NY: Barron's Educational Series, Inc., 1999.

Battaglis, Carmelo. *Dog Genetics: How to Breed Better Dogs.* Neptune, NJ: TFH Publications, 1978.

Benjamin, Carol Lea. *Mother Knows Best: The Natural Way to Train Your Dog.* New York: Howell Book House, 1985.

Lorenz, Konrad Z. *Man Meets Dog.* London and New York: Penguin Books, 1967.

Wilcox, Charlotte. *The Siberian Husky.* Mankato, MN: Capstone High-Low Books, 1999.

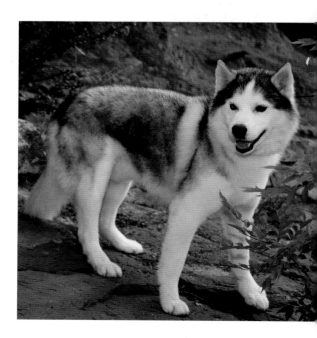

About the Author

Kerry Kern, formerly Managing Editor of the *Canine Graphic*, has written extensively on the subject of dogs. She is the author of *Rottweilers, Labrador Retrievers,* and *The New Terrier Handbook.*

A Note on Pronouns

Many dog lovers feel that the pronoun "it" is not appropriate when referring to a beloved pet. For this reason, Siberian Huskies are referred to as "he" throughout this book unless the topic specifically relates to female dogs. No gender bias is intended by this writing style.

Cover Photos

Shutterstock: front cover, back cover, inside front cover, inside back cover.

Photo Credits

Barbara Augello: page 4; Gerry Bucsis/Barbara Somerville: page 20; Seth Casteel: pages 10, 11, 22, 26, 45, 75; Kent Dannen: pages 68, 83, 93; Cheryl Ertelt: pages 28, 57; Shirley Fernandez: page 55; Daniel Johnson: pages 7, 25, 27, 46, 61, 73, 77, 81; Paws on the Run: page 50; Pets by Paulette: pages 56, 80; Shutterstock: pages 2–3, 5, 9, 17, 21, 24, 31, 32, 34, 36, 40, 53, 54, 69, 76, 82; Connie Summers: pages 12, 15, 16, 18, 19, 33, 39, 47, 49, 62, 63, 65, 66; Joan Hustace Walker: pages 52, 59, 89, 91.

All inquiries should be addressed to:
Barron's Educational Series, Inc.
250 Wireless Boulevard
Hauppauge, NY 11788
www.barronseduc.com

ISBN: 978-0-7641-4593-3

Library of Congress Catalog Card No. 2010936164

Printed in China

9 8 7 6 5 4 3 2 1

Important Note

This book discusses buying, keeping, and raising Siberian Huskies. The publisher and the author think it is important to point out that the advice and information regarding Siberian maintenance applies to healthy, normally developed animals. Anyone who buys an adult Siberian or adopts one from an animal shelter must consider that the animal may have behavioral problems and may, for example, bite without any visible provocation. Such anxiety-biters are dangerous for the owner and for the general public.

Caution is further advised in the association of children with a Siberian, in meetings with other dogs, and in exercising the dog without a leash.